Teaching the Big Class

ADVICE FROM A HISTORY COLLEAGUE

David Vaught

Texas A&M University

Bedford/St. Martin's

Boston ◆ *New York*

For Bedford/St.Martin's

Publisher for History: Mary V. Dougherty
Executive Editor for History: William J. Lombardo
Director of Development for History: Jane Knetzger
Senior Developmental Editor: Sara Wise
Production Associate: Ashley Chalmers
Executive Marketing Manager: Jenna Bookin Barry
Project Management: Books By Design, Inc.
Text Design: Books By Design, Inc.
Cover Design: Andrea Corbin
Composition: Books By Design, Inc.
Printing and Binding: Malloy Lithography, Inc.

President: Joan E. Feinberg
Editorial Director: Denise B. Wydra
Director of Marketing: Karen R. Soeltz
Director of Production: Susan W. Brown
Associate Director of Editorial Production: Elise S. Kaiser
Manager, Publishing Services: Emily Berleth

Library of Congress Control Number: 2010932773

Manufactured in the United States of America.

5 4 3 2 1 0
f e d c b a

For information, write: Bedford/St. Martin's, 75 Arlington Street, Boston, MA 02116
(617-399-4000)

ISBN-10: 0-312-57145-3
ISBN-13: 978-0-312-57145-0

Preface

Teaching the Big Class is a practical guide for instructors at large universities. While the book is intended primarily for historians who are new to the lecture hall, college teachers of all disciplines and ranks facing the challenge of introductory survey courses with huge enrollments will find it a valuable resource. The challenge instructors face can be daunting. A growing body of research over several decades suggests that undergraduate students learn best in active, cooperative, and collaborative environments—that is, in small classes where faculty members can give them close attention. Yet large lecture courses continue to be a fact of life at most four-year public universities. The disjunction between theory and reality often creates low expectations, frustration, and an underlying sense of futility. If, by definition, the sheer size and anonymity of large classes mitigates against effective learning, then teaching the survey seems at best a necessary evil, and efforts to improve one's teaching a lost cause.

This book rejects that premise and argues instead that teaching large classes can be stimulating, rewarding, *and* effective. Concise and user-friendly, it offers advice on how to survive, indeed thrive, in large classroom settings. Preparing syllabi, selecting required readings, drafting and delivering lectures, incorporating technology, conducting writing workshops, developing discussion strategies, putting together multiple-choice exams, and working with teaching assistants are among the many subjects covered. Above all, *Teaching the Big Class* takes a personal approach—colleague to colleague—not a theoretical or technical one. It emphasizes my own experiences as a teacher, faculty member, and department administrator, as well as those of several peers interviewed at large public universities around the country.

The profession is full of pressure and anxiety to publish, get tenure, perform university service, and grapple with departmental politics. For novice instructors, the large survey class often compounds that pressure and anxiety. It does not have to be that way. With the right approach, teaching the big class can be one of the biggest thrills of one's career.

Acknowledgments

Numerous colleagues, dozens of teaching assistants, and thousands of students—some of whom appear in this book under pseudonyms—have greatly influenced my teaching over the years. Thank you, one and all. Special thanks to Troy Bickham for his helpful comments on the manuscript. At Bedford/St. Martin's, Bill Lombardo enthusiastically supported this project from the outset, and Sara Wise and Judith Riotto enhanced the quality of the final product substantially. Most important, I thank my family. When I come home at the end of the day, my wife, Ethel, often asks me, "What's new and exciting in the world of history?" More than a few of those stories are retold in this book. My daughter, Diana, teaches me about life and love every day. I dedicate this book to her.

Contents

Introduction

In the fall of 1997, my first semester as an assistant professor at Texas A&M University, I found myself standing in a daze before a mass of first-year students—right in the middle of my lecture on the Great Awakening. Time, it seemed, had come to a standstill, so I could take stock of my surroundings. The long rows of chairs, stacked one on top of the other, extended as far back as I could see to the outer reaches of ANIN 215, a huge, majestic lecture hall in the center of campus. The whole room funneled steeply downward so that all two hundred chairs faced directly toward me. This must have been what it was like on the floor of the Roman Colosseum, awaiting execution, I thought to myself. The seats in the first three and back five rows were crammed full of students, but the rest in between were half empty (it would not have occurred to me to think of them as half full).

Out of the corner of my eye, I spotted a student flipping through the pages of the campus newspaper. Ten rows up, straight ahead, two others were whispering back and forth to each other and giggling, even though I was looking right at them. Several more were eating, sleeping, doing homework for another class, passing personal notes to each other, turning around every few moments to check the clock, or simply staring off into space. (Today, they would also be texting on their cell phones or playing online games on their laptops.) Nobody seemed to be taking notes on my lecture, even though I had stressed the need to do so in the syllabus and over and over again in class. The knot in my stomach grew larger, tighter, and increasingly painful, and the white long-sleeved shirt underneath my tweed jacket and carefully chosen matching tie was soaked in sweat. Am I going to have to run to the bathroom to throw up, I wondered, as I had four weeks earlier, just minutes before the first day of class? After what seemed an eternity but was probably only a few seconds, I finally gathered myself together and trudged on to the next point, but not before having a great awakening of my own: Who am I kidding? I can't teach. I suck.

These sorts of out-of-body experiences and debilitating moments of self-doubt have tormented instructors of large introductory courses probably since lecturers at medieval universities imparted knowledge to their students, if not before. I cannot vouch for my predecessors from the High Middle Ages, but the deep feelings of inadequacy stayed with me long after class was over. They haunted me on the walk back to my department, in my office for the rest of the day, on my way home in the car, when I tried to go to sleep that night, and for several days thereafter. And of course, the whole cycle could start over again at any time on Monday, Wednesday, or Friday between 9:10 and 10:00 in the morning. The whole semester seemed like a cross between *Groundhog Day* and *The Twilight Zone*.

Like most new faculty, very little in my graduate school experience had prepared me for this. As a teaching assistant at the University of California, Davis, I had observed many professors lecture day in and day out and thought, How hard could this be? My fellow TAs and I took great pleasure in criticizing the content of their lectures ("Can you believe he spent a whole hour on Warren G. Harding and Calvin Coolidge?") and making fun of their deliveries ("Man, he had us all in a coma!"), but we rarely, if ever, talked with them or among ourselves about practices, methods, and philosophies, let alone the nuts and bolts of putting a course together. A more substantial teaching apprenticeship seemed unnecessary, we all thought. Learning how to teach somehow just happened, perhaps by osmosis. By the time I started my tenure-track job, I had taught two small summer session courses on my own, finished my dissertation, published a couple of articles, and dazzled the search committee with my pedagogical insights. I was riding high. What more did I need to teach HIST 105 to a couple of hundred freshmen? A great deal, as it turned out. A great deal, indeed.

It does not have to happen this way.

That is the central premise of *Teaching the Big Class*. Simply put, the book is a practical guide for instructors at large universities. While it is intended primarily for historians who are new to the large lecture hall, college teachers of all disciplines and ranks facing the challenge of introductory survey courses with huge enrollments will find it a valuable resource. That challenge can be daunting, as my own painful experience demonstrates. The vast literature on higher education insists that undergraduate students learn best in small classes—the smaller the better—where instructors can provide active, cooperative, and collaborative environments. This sounds irrefutable, in theory. In reality, however, large lecture courses are a fact of life at most four-year public universities. What, then, are new faculty members to do? If, by definition, the sheer size and anonymity of large classes mitigates against effective learning, then trying to improve one's teaching seems an exercise in futility. This sequence of realizations invariably creates low expectations and frustration. It is little wonder, therefore, that new instructors are often thrown into the classroom to sink or swim on their own and that their more experienced colleagues are often reluctant to discuss strategies, methods, and concerns among themselves.

This book seeks to jump-start these discussions. It emphasizes that teaching large classes can, in fact, be stimulating, rewarding, *and* effective. Concise and user-friendly, it offers advice not only on how to survive in so-called factory schools, but also on how to *thrive* in such large schools. Among the many subjects covered are preparing syllabi; selecting required readings; drafting and delivering lectures; incorporating technology (or not); conducting writing, reading, and note-taking workshops; developing discussion strategies; putting together multiple-choice exams; and working with (or without) teaching assistants. Above all, *Teaching the Big Class* takes a personal approach—colleague to colleague—not a theoretical or technical one. It is based primarily on my own experiences as a teacher, faculty member, and department administrator, as well as my observations and interviews of several peers at large public universities around the country. The profession is full of pressure and anxiety to publish, get tenure, perform university service, and play the game of departmental politics. For many novice, midcareer, and senior professors alike, the large survey class compounds that pressure and anxiety. Again, *it does not have to be this way*. With the right approach and the right attitude, teaching the big class can be a big opportunity and perhaps even one of the biggest thrills of one's career.

In a sense, I have been writing this book for some time now. Several years ago, I developed a graduate seminar on professional development that I teach regularly. About half the course is devoted to undergraduate teaching, stressing practice over theory. We have extensive discussions, mock lectures, and roundtables with several other faculty members. I also teach the U.S. history survey almost every semester, which involves, in essence, teaching my teaching assistants how to teach. Among my duties as associate department head—a position I've held since 2006—I hire and supervise all of our temporary instructors (about a dozen in all in any given year), observe them in the classroom, and evaluate their lecturing, syllabi, grading, and overall performance. I offer the same service to new assistant professors in my department, most of whom are eager, though anxious, to take advantage of it.

Many of the new teachers to our campus come from small liberal arts colleges and private universities. It is increasingly the case, in fact, that universities such as Texas A&M are hiring young PhD's from Ivy League schools and similar institutions who have never been in a classroom—undergraduate or graduate—of more than ten or fifteen people. Not surprisingly, they often have a very difficult time adjusting to the realities of teaching at a place like Texas A&M, which has forty-eight thousand undergraduates—which is to say, large and sometimes very large survey classes of 150 to three hundred students.

This book, then, gives me the opportunity to formalize what I already do in my department on an informal basis—offer advice to graduate students, adjuncts, new faculty, and even more seasoned colleagues on how to teach history at large public universities. There are several "how to" guides for college instructors available. But even the best among them—Ken Bain's *What the Best College Teachers Do*, Peter Filene's *The Joy of Teaching*, and James Lang's *On Course*—offer very little for those of us who teach in "factory" schools.[1] With my love of the large lecture hall and considerable experience helping others learn to love the large lecture hall, my hope is that I have produced a book that proves useful to instructors at large universities across the country.

Teaching the Big Class is practical in purpose, candid in assessment, and conversational in style. In the interest of full disclosure, I must note that I am not well versed in the formal literature of higher education. Outcome assessment, learning communities, inquiry-based instruction, and other cutting-edge pedagogies have their place, to be sure. But it has been my experience that these approaches, however nuanced and complex, are more likely to confuse new teachers than to help them, especially those trying to find their way in introductory survey courses with hundreds of students. In finding my way since that rough start in ANIN 215 my first semester, I have learned that teaching is an ongoing and uneven process of discovery. It varies tremendously from one individual to the next in style, practice, substance, and philosophy. There is no single model for success. It is in that spirit that I present this book. It offers no hard and fast rules, no ironclad truths, and no abstract theory—just advice from a colleague to help you find your way.[2]

Notes

1. Ken Bain, *What the Best College Teachers Do* (Cambridge, Mass.: Harvard University Press, 2004); Peter Filene, *The Joy of Teaching: A Practical Guide for New College Instructors* (Chapel Hill: University of North Carolina Press, 2005); and James M. Lang, *On Course: A Week-by-Week Guide to Your First Semester of College Teaching* (Cambridge, Mass.: Harvard University Press, 2008).
2. For a similar approach, see Patrick Allitt, *I'm the Teacher, You're the Student: A Semester in the University Classroom* (Philadelphia: University of Pennsylvania Press, 2004).

CHAPTER 1

Before the Semester Begins

Large is not small. "Duh," my fifteen-year-old daughter would say. The differences between, for example, a class of three hundred and a class of twenty-five may at first seem self-evident. Twelve times as many students will be seated in front of you each and every class period. You will have to speak louder, distribute more copies of the syllabus, answer more questions, and calculate a lot more final grades. Field trips are out. Good luck learning their names. When your jokes are funny, the auditorium will echo in laughter, but should they fall flat, the silence will be deafening.

Other differences, not quite so obvious, will become readily apparent soon enough. When attendance is low in a class of twenty-five, you may not be bothered by it or even notice, but a half-empty lecture hall has the feel of a funeral parlor. In a small class, you can "wing it" on occasion, but try coming in unprepared before three hundred freshmen and sophomores and see how far you get. When the bookstore runs out of one of your required readings a week before the paper is due, you will have a veritable crisis on your hands in a large class, a mere inconvenience in a small one. There will be more ringing cell phones interrupting your lectures, more late arrivals and early departures, more complaints from disgruntled students (and more reasons to be disgruntled), more cheating during exams, and more plagiarizing on papers in a large class. Many more students will request makeups and extensions, extra credit, midsemester grade estimates ("What do I need on this paper to raise my average to a B?"), and alternative times for the final exam ("I have three other exams on that day"). The number of grandmothers who will pass away over the course of the semester—all, coincidentally, just prior to scheduled exams—will far exceed the per capita average (but far fewer, if any, grandfathers will die, for reasons I have never quite understood). You will need more patience, a much thicker skin, and to think faster on your feet. For all your efforts, however, you will in all likelihood receive significantly lower student evaluation scores.

Still other differences will be more subtle and complex. In contrast to small upper-division courses, which are packed with majors from history and other liberal arts, the large required introductory survey will be a cross section of the entire student body. In absolute numbers, you may actually have fewer history majors in the large class than in the small class. There will be dozens of other majors, from engineering and chemistry to business and computer science (and several you will not even recognize). You will have your share of athletes, a broad range of races and ethnicities, career-minded students, rebellious students, homesick students, first-generation college students, fraternity brothers, sorority sisters, graduates of top-of-the-line suburban high schools, and graduates from impoverished urban or rural school districts—the whole spectrum, in other words, sitting right in your class. This presents a number of perplexing questions for approaching the course. How rigorous should it be? What readings are appropriate? How much writing? How many exams? What kinds of exams? How much knowledge of the subject should you assume of students? How and at what level should you pitch your lectures?

Just a few more differences before I stop. A small class gives teachers much greater flexibility and more room to experiment. Over the course of the semester, they have the luxury of varying their teaching techniques and offering students a wide range of assignments to test their skills and knowledge multiple times and in multiple ways.[1] A large class, in sharp contrast, demands structure, repetition, and symmetry. Instructors of large classes also need to train, guide, and supervise their teaching assistants, stay on top of the course schedule at all times, understand all the pertinent university rules and regulations, and be ready to handle unforeseen problems as they arise (as they most certainly will). In short, you are not only a teacher in a large class; you are also a manager.

The keys to being a successful teacher-manager are preparation, preparation, and more preparation, most of which can and should be done before the semester begins—well before. If you walk into your office a few days before class starts expecting to keep a few days ahead of your students for the rest of the term, you will be in for a rude awakening. You will find yourself swamped in work and way behind before you know what hits you. The importance of budgeting your time cannot be overstated with three hundred students depending on you to maintain a steady course. Large is not small, indeed.

Getting Started

Preparation begins, especially for new hires, by asking colleagues if they would be willing to share their syllabi. Most will be flattered that you asked and eager to tell you how things are done. The problem in a department as large as mine (approaching fifty faculty members, sixty with adjuncts) is that you are likely to get widely varying responses as to how things are done. Nonetheless, your colleagues still may have valuable information, the kind that cannot be found in the university catalog. At Texas A&M, for example, the Wednesday before Thanksgiving has become, for better or for worse, an unofficial holiday. Though you may feel obligated to uphold standards, your classroom will be near empty if you try to hold class. Also, because the campus is so large, classes are scheduled twenty minutes apart, rather than the customary ten, which makes for very odd, unintuitive starting and finishing times. (I still find them confusing.) It is prudent, therefore, to write "MWF 12:40 to 1:30" on the top of your syllabus as a reminder for you and your students. Beyond these sorts of helpful tidbits, however, you will likely find little consensus among your new colleagues on how to prepare your course.

My best piece of advice is simply "less is best," especially the first time around for a new teacher in a big class. If you find yourself trying to decide between less reading or more reading, choose less. More assignments or fewer assignments? Choose fewer. A longer or a shorter lecture? Shorter. Give yourself a chance to learn the ropes before getting more adventurous, and give your students a chance to get comfortable with you. This is a long-term, trial-and-error process. There will be plenty of opportunities to revise the course in the semesters ahead. After sifting through all the information and advice you have gathered, your instincts and experience will, in the end, be your best guides. Pack rats who have long been ridiculed by spouses, partners, and others for keeping class notes from their undergraduate and graduate school days will now reap the rewards and enjoy sweet revenge. I used my old notes as a starting point for almost all of my first lectures.

Preparation then proceeds by getting yourself two calendars—one blank with plenty of room to write on, the other your institution's academic calendar for the semester. Transcribe the pertinent bits of information from the institution's calendar to the blank calendar—first and last days of class, holidays, add/drop deadlines, day and time of your final exam, and the day when final grades are due. Make no assumptions. Before my first semester, for example, I noticed, with great puzzlement, that class was scheduled to begin on Labor Day. Surely there must be some mistake, I thought, so I phoned my department head to alert her. Texas, she responded in so many words, is not California. The following semester I learned, through a similar process, that Good Friday is a university holiday even though Labor Day is not.

With the bare bones of a schedule now in front of you, it is time to begin thinking more specifically about the course. Keep in mind your audience: most likely young, fresh-out-of-high-school, away-from-home-for-the-first-time, impressionable students. Do you remember what it was like to be eighteen or nineteen years old in your first year in college? If you were like most students, you struggled with apathy, inattention, forgetfulness, self-doubt, self-pity, self-image, self-control, self-discipline, self-indulgence, self-respect, and/or self-awareness. How does one possibly handle three hundred freshmen and sophomores, each with this rather frightening profile, let alone engage them in some meaningful way? The answer is with structure—and the more and the tighter, the better. Students thrive on structure, and so will you.

Creating Your Syllabus

The syllabus puts the design of your course into concrete form. Be sure to check your university's Web site for minimum requirements, but realize that as long as you include no statements contrary to university rules (regarding attendance, approved absences, etc.), the syllabus is yours for the making. Take advantage. Craft the syllabus in your own image. Think of it not only as a roadmap for the semester, but as the students' introduction to the course, to the subject matter, and most important, to you. Set the tone, establish your priorities, and showcase your expertise and enthusiasm. The most useful way for me to demonstrate this approach, I think, is to discuss an actual syllabus—my own for HIST 106, "History of the United States from 1877"—rather than a generic one full of abstractions. In this way, I can take you through my decision making step-by-step, as well as consider other options and offer recommendations. (See the syllabus in its entirety in Appendix A.)

Please note that this particular course meets for fifty minutes three times a week, in the lecture hall on Monday and Wednesday, and in small discussion sections during the remainder of the week. Each discussion section has twenty-five students and is taught by one of six graduate assistants. At Texas A&M, as at many large public universities, some of the other U.S. survey courses do not have discussion sections, though instructors are provided with a grader. This format sometimes calls for different strategies in the planning of the course, and I will make note of them as we proceed.[2]

Two general comments before diving in. You will not find in my syllabus any references to extra credit, review sessions, or options to throw out the lowest grade on an exam or paper. Students adore these sorts of grade pick-me-ups because high schools offer them in abundance. Asking for extra credit, in fact, seems to go all the way back to kindergarten. My daughter has received grades of 110 or higher for as long as I can remember. But this is not high school, let alone kindergarten. This is college. And part of college is learning to take responsibility for the here and now, without the safety net of extra credit always there to help you atone for your sins. The good students, moreover, have learned to resent extra credit, review sessions, and other such gimmicks because they know they only benefit the slackers—those who have fallen behind with the notes, reading, and discussions. The bottom line: If you treat students like they are still in high school, then they will act like they are still in high school.

Think about the tone and the length of the syllabus as well before you get started. I prefer a neutral tone—not too rah-rah, not too drill-sergeant-like. I try to reveal my enthusiasm for the subject more by what I say than how I say it, and I pick my times to lay down the law. Too many what-not-to-do's in capital letters with exclamation points will turn students off and thus defeat the purpose. They will peg you as just another crabby teacher and, more likely than not, tune out your instructions.

As for length, some people maintain that the shorter the syllabus, the more likely students will read it—and there is some truth to that, to be sure. Nonetheless, to provide students an immediate sense of what the course will cover, what work is expected of them, and how their performance will be evaluated, I prefer to err on the side of too much information. A well-prepared, comprehensive syllabus also tells students that you are careful, well organized, conscientious, and serious about teaching. Even a perfect syllabus is not foolproof, however. In a huge class of eighteen- and nineteen-year-olds, no matter how much you try to minimize misunderstandings about due dates, grading criteria, attendance, missed exams, late papers, etc., at least a third—that means one hundred students in this class—will claim ignorance at some time during the semester and ask you to explain something you have already explained dozens of times. Guaranteed. Accept it, explain it again, and move on.[3]

The syllabus begins with the customary information:

History of the United States from 1877

Class, Instructor, and TA Information

Class Meetings: MW 12:40 to 1:30, in CHEM 100, + your
   scheduled discussion section
Office: 314B HIST
Phone: 555-5555
Office Hours: M 11:00 to 12:00, W 2:00 to 3:00, and by
   appointment
Virtual Office Hours: vaught@college.edu

[Teaching assistants, listed with name, e-mail addresses, office, office hours]

Nothing too complicated here, of course. On the first day of class, I briefly explain the concept of the discussion section (knowing that the TAs will elaborate later). To provide students greater access to you, and to demonstrate to them your desire to be accessible, schedule your office hours on different days and at different times (the same applies for teaching assistants). While some teaching guidebooks advise instructors to consider giving students their home (or cell) phone number as a symbolic gesture of openness, I would think long and hard about sharing it with a large class.[4] As for "virtual office hours," I tell students to sit tight if I do not reply to e-mail right away and that they normally will hear back from me by the end of the day.

Course Description and Objectives

This course surveys modern American history from the latter third of the nineteenth century to the present, using three complementary approaches: lecture, reading, and discussion. We will explore economic, social, cultural, and political developments, paying close attention to regional variations and the different experiences of whites and blacks, men and women, natives and immigrants, and workers and farmers. The objective is to be neither comprehensive nor definitive, but to introduce students to the key themes, events, and personalities of the period and to develop their critical thinking, writing, reading, and note-taking skills. Prerequisites: none.

Try to be provocative but brief. Students will not pay much attention to long, rambling course descriptions (would you?). State legislatures increasingly want to require a "learning outcomes" section on course syllabi, though Texas A&M only "recommends" one at this point. In a recertification exercise a couple of years ago, the history department (well, me, actually, in my administrative capacity) devised a series of standardized learning outcomes for our courses, as follows:

During the semester, students will:

1. Expand their knowledge of the human condition and human cultures in the context of the subject matter of the course.
2. Enhance their abilities to reason logically and respond critically to a wide range of historical evidence, both primary and secondary.

3. Acquire an understanding of the intellectual demands required of historians through their own critical analysis — thinking, reading, listening, speaking, and writing.
4. Gain an appreciation of history as both a field of knowledge and a creative process.
5. Broaden their awareness of the scope and variety of contemporary and historical issues and interpretations.
6. Learn to understand these issues and interpretations in their historical and social contexts.
7. Develop the ability to apply knowledge of diverse backgrounds and cultures to their personal lives and studies.

The time will come, sooner rather than later no doubt, when we will be told to stamp these objectives across the front of all our syllabi. Why, I will never quite understand. Perhaps I am ignorant, but I fail to see what these sorts of (dare I say, vacuous) statements add to a course, for students or instructors. So much for clarity and originality. But such is life at a public university.

Required Readings (available at the bookstore)

Thomas Bell, *Out of This Furnace: A Novel of Immigrant Labor in America*

John Kasson, *Amusing the Million: Coney Island at the Turn of the Century*

Sinclair Lewis, *Babbitt*

Yoshiko Uchida, *Desert Exile: The Uprooting of a Japanese-American Family*

Melba Pattillo Beals, *Warriors Don't Cry: A Searing Memoir of the Battle to Integrate Little Rock's Central High*

Philip Caputo, *A Rumor of War*

OPTIONAL TEXT: James A. Henretta, David Brody, and Lynn Dumenil, *America: A Concise History*, 3rd ed.

As is evident, I am a book person. Students simply do not read enough books anymore. Other instructors prefer articles, readers, or document collections, which are fine, but there is something about seeing students before class or outside on campus reading one of the books I have assigned that warms my heart. The right books can really make the class.

Choosing the right books, however, is no easy task. In that first infamous semester of mine at Texas A&M, I assigned six cutting-edge monographs with my colleagues more in mind than my students. (Boy, this will impress them, I thought.) The first was William Cronon's *Changes in the Land: Indians, Colonists, and the Ecology of New England*, a fabulous book, but decisively not right for HIST 105. My guess is that maybe fifty of the two hundred students managed to read through to the end, even fewer with much comprehension. The rest of the books fared no better, all of which made papers and exams exceedingly difficult (for them and for me) and the semester itself that much more of a struggle (again, for all of us). The lesson: Strive to challenge but not frustrate your students with the course reading. It can be a fine line, to say the least. I have learned to choose books that are, above all else, readable, engaging, and consistent with the goals of breadth and diversity set forth in the course description. For HIST 106, I have found that the three firsthand accounts (Uchida, Beals, and Caputo), two novels (Bell and Lewis), and one thin monograph with great photographs (Kasson) that make up my reading list work very well. I am far less confident, I confess, in the books I assign for the first half of the survey, even after endless conversations with colleagues, one of which began back in graduate school and continues to this day.

The appropriate amount of reading is also tough to gauge. My standard advice to newly hired instructors at Texas A&M, in accordance with my when-in-doubt-do-less philosophy, is to start with a textbook and three additional readings and then branch out from there in subsequent semesters as your confidence grows. Six books for a survey course is at the high end of the scale in my department, but that number is balanced by making the textbook optional. I prefer to have students use the textbook primarily as a reference source. The lectures are far more important; indeed, the textbook is not covered on the exams. About half the students, on average, purchase it to read up on subjects that they either missed or did not fully understand in lecture.

On more practical matters, be sure to order your books by the deadline, which is usually set well before the start of the semester. Check your campus bookstore to see if your books are on the shelf a couple of weeks before class starts, and advise your students to purchase them early, before the bookstore clears their shelves (about halfway through the term at Texas A&M, but this will vary by institution). Finally, order desk copies for your teaching assistants. This can usually be done on the publisher's Web site.

Assessment

All graded assignments and exams must be completed to earn a passing grade.

First Exam	10%
Second Exam	15%
Final Exam	25%
First Paper	15%
Second Paper	25%
Discussion	10%

One of the reasons that I am so set on six books is that six works perfectly with the way the course is structured. I divide the course into thirds, each with the same number of lectures (9), discussions (4), books (2), and exams (1). This approach establishes a rhythm to the semester, which gives young students, who have varying levels of knowledge and maturity, a chance to adjust to the demands of the class at their own pace. The teaching assistants and I try our best at the outset to explain what to expect with regard to exams, papers, and discussions. But we can do this in the abstract until we are blue in the face; in most cases, students have to actually take an exam, write a paper, and participate in discussion before they get the hang of it. For some, it may take two times around the track. But they know, because we tell them repeatedly, that the second and third sections of the course will proceed along exactly the same lines as the first.

Assessment, in the scheme of my syllabus, then reinforces this tight, symmetrical structure. Course grades, especially for the survey, should take into account the amount of growth and development a student shows over the course of a semester. If all three exams are weighted equally, a low grade on the first one can bury the student and kill their confidence right then and there by not giving them an opportunity to learn from their mistakes. The same holds true for the first paper. In contrast, if the percentages are staggered to build improvement directly into the grade scale, then students who start badly, for whatever reason, get a second chance. Many dozens of students in my survey courses over the years have started with a D or an F on the first exam or paper but ended up, with a lot of hard work, doing quite well, earning a B or even an A. The objective is not to make things easy for students, but to give them plenty of opportunity to succeed.

The statement "All graded assignments and exams must be completed to earn a passing grade" is meant to discourage students who, after calculating their grade, think they can skip the second paper or third exam and still get a passing grade. A few still try every semester, however (sigh).

Discussions

In the third hour of every week, students will meet in small discussion sections to explore issues and problems raised by the readings and to develop critical thinking, reading, and writing skills. (Some of you meet on Wednesdays, some on Thursdays, and some on Fridays.) Though your TA will facilitate these discussions, the burden of their success or usefulness is on you. It is very important, therefore, that students begin reading and thinking carefully about the books *well in advance* of the day of the discussion (see schedule below). Reading guides consisting of 10 to 15 questions will be distributed approximately two weeks prior to the discussion date. Answer the questions informally (a couple or so sentences for each) and note the approximate page numbers on which you find the answers. *Make a copy of your answers for yourself, and hand the original in at the beginning of the discussion section.* This will allow you to make additions while sharing your thoughts with your classmates. The reading guides will help prepare you for discussions, which in turn will help prepare you for papers and exams. Small discussion sections are rare at large universities like this one. Take advantage of this opportunity!

This section of the syllabus is too long both visually and substantively, but I do not really expect the students to absorb it all at first. I know from experience, in fact, that no matter how carefully

I explain these procedures either in the syllabus or in class, many students will not come prepared in the prescribed manner for the first discussion. This is one of those instances when students simply have to go through the process themselves the first time before figuring it all out. I instruct my TAs to be lenient with them at first, especially with making two copies of the reading guides and turning them in on time. Most students are ready the next time around.

The reading guides are an important, if ungraded, part of the course. Education theorists call them "low-stakes assignments," designed not as an end in themselves, but as a means to encourage students to grapple with the reading and develop their ideas *prior* to the discussion.[5] The questions are in chronological order as students read through the book; some are factual, while others are more thematic and conceptual. They are designed to help students maintain their focus and, as the instructions indicate, to help them prepare for papers and exams. (See Appendix B for examples of my reading guides. See Chapter 3 for more explanation of the discussion component of the course.) For now, let me just say that the reading guides really do work. The alternative—students walking into their sections with no preparation other than having read (or not read) the book—really does not work.

Without teaching assistants, discussions are much more difficult, of course. But I still offer a variant of what is outlined above. In fact, I used the reading guide system for years in semesters when I had only one grader, and then I adapted it to the format with formal discussion sections. Even when it is just the grader and me in the lecture hall, I still set aside six full class periods for discussion in the course schedule, one for each book. We do not proceed with me at the podium asking questions to all three hundred students at the same time (which never works very well). Instead, I have the students break up into dozens of small groups of five or six (of their own choosing) to discuss the reading guide questions among themselves. While they are sprawled out across the lecture hall, my grader and I roam from group to group answering as many questions as we can. I tell them they can leave whenever they are finished, and many—perhaps half—are out on the street in twenty minutes. But those who take it seriously welcome the opportunity to explore issues and problems raised by the readings with their peers and stay the whole period. The system is far from perfect.

But it demonstrates that with a little ingenuity, instructors can sometimes make big classes seem small.[6]

Papers

1. First Paper: 15% of final grade
    A 3-page analytical essay based primarily on *one* of the first three required readings, due as follows:

    Bell, *Out of This Furnace*, due Feb. 2
    Kasson, *Amusing the Million*, due Feb. 16
    Lewis, *Babbitt*, due March 9

2. Second Paper: 25% of final grade
    A 3-page analytical essay based primarily on *one* of the three remaining required readings, due as follows:

    Uchida, *Desert Exile*, due March 30
    Beals, *Warriors Don't Cry*, due April 20
    Caputo, *A Rumor of War*, due May 4

Topics will be distributed approximately two weeks prior to the due date. It is always wise to keep a copy of each written assignment until you receive your final grade. *When turning in papers, students should submit both paper and electronic copies to their teaching assistants.*

Ideally, I would assign three short papers, both for pedagogical purposes and to fit the three-fold structure of the course. But three would place too much of a burden on the graders. In my department, teaching assistants are paid for twenty hours a week (on average), and it is the instructor's responsibility not to overwork them. The papers still follow the same logic already established in the syllabus: symmetry, in that the procedure for the second paper is exactly the same as the first one; and the built-in improvement factor, with the second paper worth considerably more than the first. In addition, students get to choose which books they want to write about from each group of three. This also has the advantage of staggering the due dates for the papers so that the teaching assistants do not have to grade them all at once—though, in truth, at least half the students will wait for the third option every time.

There are additional ways to let students know that you value good writing. Many of them every semester will complain after receiving a disappointing grade that grammar, spelling, and composition should not count in history because writing is the domain of the English department. One way to begin launching a counter-attack against this fallacy is to stress the importance of clear, thoughtful writing on your syllabus. Even the casual reader of my syllabus, for example, will notice the two-page "Guidelines for Writing Papers" at the end. And if they look a little closer, they will find two writing workshops in the course schedule. (See Chapter 3 for descriptions.)

Assigning papers gets more complicated when there are no discussion sections simply because there are fewer graders—just the one—in this format. In fact, even two papers are too much for one grader. I make the second paper optional in this case. Students who are satisfied with their grade on the first paper may choose to make it the full 40 percent of the final grade. They will often ask if a lower grade on the second paper will bring the total grade down, to which I always answer no. I am the first to admit that pedagogically, two papers are much better than one. The real learning takes place with the second paper, when students are able to apply the detailed feedback they received on the first. But with two or three hundred students in the class, the grader, at twenty hours a week, simply does not have the time for two papers in addition to his or her other duties.

There is another option. You, the instructor, could grade half the papers. This poses a real, sometimes profound, professional dilemma, especially for newly hired teachers who, of course, want to be conscientious: Is it in your best interest to read all those papers? This dilemma, I cannot stress enough, needs to be resolved *before* the semester starts, *before* you construct your syllabus. The answer depends in part on what your department and, by extension, your institution expect of you. At research institutions, such as Texas A&M, the bottom line is that professors are not paid to grade freshmen papers, no matter how crass that may sound. The many hours that it would take to grade them are better spent on professors' own research. As associate department head, I advise our adjunct professors, following the same logic, not to spend huge chunks of their time grading papers. They, of course, not only have publishing pressures of their own; they also are usually on the job market. These realities, unfortunately, often go unspoken in the first years on the job, but it is your responsibility to figure out what your obligations are in the classroom. Tough choices have to be made when teaching the big class, and this is one of the tougher ones. Make it right away.

I have my students turn in electronic copies of their papers so that teaching assistants, when they feel it necessary, can forward them to turnitin.com, an antiplagiarism online service that scans papers against many Internet sources, including other papers submitted to the site. (See Chapter 3 for more on plagiarism, as well as designing effective paper topics and grading the papers themselves.)

Exams

All three exams (February 18, 19, or 20; April 1, 2, or 3; and May 11) will be closed-book and closed-note and will cover *all* lectures and readings. Each exam will have two parts. Part I will consist of 30 multiple-choice/true-false questions from the lectures, and Part II will be one essay question based on the pertinent books (Bell and Kasson for Exam I, Lewis and Uchida for Exam II, and Beals and Caputo for Exam III). Part I will count for 60 percent of the exam grade, and Part II will be worth 40 percent. Please note that Part I will cover the lectures, *not* the textbook. This makes it imperative that you attend class regularly and read the books carefully. There will be NO MAKEUPS except for students with university-excused absences (please see http://student-rules.tamu.edu/rule07.htm for current policy on university-excused absences). It is the responsibility of the student to confer with his/her teaching assistant to arrange a day for the makeup exam.

Exams, like papers, involve pedagogical, practical, and professional considerations. The size of the class, the amount of grading assistance, and how you decide to budget your time between teaching, research, and service obligations go a long way toward determining the kinds of questions you can ask. I think it is fair to say that in a perfect world, we would all give essay exams. No other type of exam better enables instructors to judge students' abilities to organize, integrate, and interpret the material and to express themselves in their own words. This is especially true, I think, on the portion of an exam that covers the course readings.

When I have multiple teaching assistants for a large class, my solution is to give hybrid exams. The first part consists of thirty multiple-choice and true-false questions, and the second part is an essay question on one of the two books pertaining to that portion of the course. The objective questions do not come from a textbook test bank or any other such source. I write them based directly on my lectures. They cover not the nitty-gritty details, facts, and dates, but broad themes and concepts, as suggested by the lecture outlines (see Appendix C for sample outlines). The essay questions, on the other hand, are the domain of the teaching assistants, who construct their own questions (with my assistance) based on the content or emphasis of the discussions that took place in their particular sections. Because of the fifty-minute class period, students only have time for one essay after completing the objective part of the exam. How, then, do we ensure that they read both books and come prepared to answer questions on both? We do not tell them in advance which book will be on the exam. How unfair, they say. How clever, we tell each other.

With just one grader, however, the exams are entirely objective—sixty multiple-choice and true-false questions: forty straight from the lectures, ten from each of the two pertinent books. In this format, it is simply not feasible to spend the amount of time needed to grade essays, especially since I assign the two take-home papers. One possibility, which many in my department prefer, is to forgo the take-homes and have an essay component to the exams instead. Each to his own, but I think the take-homes provide a much better learning experience. Good multiple-choice questions, while easy to grade (the machine does all the work), are very difficult to write (see Chapter 3).[7]

Briefly, with regard to makeups: At my university—and I am guessing at yours as well—rules covering university-excused absences (death in the student's family, injury or illness, court appearance, religious holy days, etc.) are formal, detailed, and readily available. You should, of course, familiarize yourself with them. That is all straightforward. But what do you do when a student approaches you at the end of lecture (when you are exhausted) and says, "Professor, my grandmother died last week, and I couldn't take the exam because I went to her funeral. Can I take it later this week?" Are you going to look her in the eyes (which by now are beginning to tear up) and tell her, "No, not without the required documentation"? Of course not. Even if it is the fifth such death in this class that month, you have no real choice but to schedule a makeup. I made fun of the ubiquitous dead-grandmother excuse earlier in this chapter, but the joke is really on us, the instructors. The savvy student knows that the dead-grandmother routine works every time. No rules, regulations, or procedures can beat it.

Attendance and Late Papers

Attendance in lecture and discussion section will be taken on a random basis at least six or seven times throughout the semester. You will not be penalized for *two* unexcused absences, but on the *third* and subsequent unexcused absences, your grade for the course will drop a full notch (i.e., from an A to a B, B to a C, etc.). Papers that are submitted late will receive a grade of zero except in the case of university-excused absences or by prior arrangement with the instructor or teaching assistant.

Please see http://student-rules.tamu.edu/rule07.htm for the current policy on university-excused absences. For illness- or injury-related absences of fewer than three days, a note from a health care professional confirming date and time of visit will be required in order to count the absence as university-excused; for absences of three days or more, the note must also contain the medical professional's confirmation that absence from class was necessary (see Rule 7.1.6.1).

To take or not to take—that is the question with regard to attendance. On the one hand, you tell yourself, these are adults. If they do not want to come to class, who am I to make them—their mother? Calling roll, sending around a sign-in sheet, assigned seating—it all seems so petty and draconian, not to mention time-consuming for the teaching assistant. That is how I proceeded my first couple of years—no attendance. I gradually learned that having no attendance policy meant lecturing to half-empty auditoriums at times, especially after spring break when the weather starts to warm up. Where would I have rather been when I was eighteen, I had to ask myself honestly, out on the quad soaking up some rays with my friends, or in HIST 106? So, for the next couple of years, I took attendance. But taking attendance in the lecture hall, I found, is hardly an exact science. When my teaching assistant, who relied on a sign-in sheet, reported that J. Paul Student missed four classes, I did not know what to do. If I followed the letter of the syllabus, I was supposed to knock his grade down a notch. But how could I be confident enough with a sign-in sheet (or any other method, for that matter) to take this rather drastic action, especially when the student swore that he only missed three lectures? To heck with this, I thought, and went back to no attendance. But if the professor does not take roll, a colleague of mine insisted shortly thereafter, it shows a lack of interest on your part in both the students and the content of the course. Damned if you do; damned if you don't.[8]

It was at this point that I developed my current—and, if I do say so myself, brilliant—policy. I lie to them—straight out. I do, on a random basis (though only a couple of times), send a sign-in sheet around. "Today," I announce with great fanfare at the beginning of class, "is an attendance day," which never fails to incite wild cheering from the masses, who declare victory simply by being there. But that is as far as it goes. When I get back to my office, I toss the signature-filled sheets on top of the heap on my desk and take no further action. This allows me to achieve the desired effect without any of the hassle. On rare occasions, a student will come in and ask me how many absences he or she has accumulated, but all I do is turn around, rustle some papers on my desk, and say, "Don't worry. You're fine." I do allow my teaching assistants to use the policy to their advantage—to take attendance (real attendance, that is) in their discussion sections as they see fit.

In all seriousness, and with all modesty aside, attendance has improved in my big classes over the years not because of any particular policy or gimmick, but because I have improved my teaching over the years. To paraphrase the voice of Shoeless Joe Jackson in *Field of Dreams*, if you teach them, they will come. Engage them, and they will not want to miss your class, regardless of what the weather is like outside (much more on that in the next chapter).

Tips

Above all, try to stay focused and relaxed! The lectures, readings, and paper topics are challenging. *Do not expect to understand them fully right off the bat.* Take careful notes and review them after each class, give yourself plenty of time to read (and reread) the books, come prepared for discussion, and do not wait until the last minute to write your papers. If you find yourself confused, *do not hesitate to come see your TA (or me) during office hours*! You might want to seek out a note-taking buddy or two in case you have to miss class.

One of my colleagues several years ago suggested that I add a short "tips" section to my syllabus for the introductory course. To the students, she explained, tips indicate that you have special insider information that you are willing to share with them, which in turn tells them that you are on their side and, of equal importance, that you are thinking about them as individuals in the otherwise impersonal setting of the lecture hall. That more than convinced me, and I have offered tips ever since. In fact, I give additional tips all the time in lecture and encourage the teaching assistants to do the same in discussion section. One of the best tips I have for HIST 106 students comes on the first day of class. I ask those who had me the previous semester for 105 (about a third of the class, usually) to raise their hands, and then I tell the others that if I were them, I would get to know one or two of these veterans, who can really give the lowdown on the class. The "tips" section, in addition, provides another opportunity to encourage students to take advantage of your (and the TAs') office hours, which you cannot do too often.

Course Schedule: Lecture and Discussion Topics

[See Appendix A, pp. 101–2, for full details.]

The class schedule is not as easy as it looks. It takes more planning than any other part of the syllabus, so leave yourself plenty of time to think it through. You already have the bare bones of a schedule from the calendar we started earlier in the chapter. It is now time to start counting. How many class periods will you have, less holidays, de facto holidays, and two exams? (Remember, the third exam takes place during finals week on a day and time designated by the university.) In my syllabus, with Texas A&M's fourteen-week semester, the answer is thirty-nine. With one discussion section per week (not counting the two exams), this breaks down to twenty-seven lectures and twelve discussions, both of which are divisible by three to fit my scheme perfectly. So far, so good. Scheduling the exams seems pretty straightforward — at the end of the first third and second third of the course. But you have to be careful not to schedule exams immediately before or after major breaks in the schedule, such as Thanksgiving and spring break. The students will hate you for it, and the small mountain of requests for makeups that will await you will be an enormous hassle. I lucked out this particular semester, but on occasion major changes have to be made.

Then there is the matter of coordinating lectures, discussions, and exams. Students are much better prepared to read the books and participate in discussions if I provide them, in advance, proper historical context in lecture. But that means, for example, that I need to finish the Industrial Revolution before they discuss *Out of This Furnace*, which then means I cannot start the course with the American Frontier, as I would prefer. Similarly, I need to get all the way through World War II before I can schedule the second exam, which limits the time I can spend on the 1920s and 1930s. These sorts of problems are compounded by the fact that discussion days are fixed — the last meeting of each week — and that exams are scheduled on discussion days (lecture days are already at a premium). I could go on and on, but I think you get my point. I hope you like a good puzzle, because the course schedule can be just as mind-boggling.[9]

If you counted carefully, you would have noticed that the course actually had only thirty-eight days, not thirty-nine. One of them—April 1, in this case—is marked TBA. I could tell you that this day was set aside so I could attend a conference, but that would be lying. You should, of course, account for the days in the schedule that you know you will miss for professional meetings, but my Monday-Wednesday schedule for this particular course does not conflict with long conference weekends. No, TBA really means ADO—A Day Off, for them and for me. I schedule TBAs—one per semester—simply to give us all a break. When I announce it two weeks or so beforehand with much drama and suspense, it brings down the house and, for many days thereafter, adds a little joy to everyone's life. Warning: This tactic is for tenured faculty only.

You will also notice that the schedule ends at Watergate, even though the course title suggests "to the present." I could tell you that I just ran out of days, but again, that would not be true. I simply do not enjoy getting up on a soapbox while standing behind the lectern in front of three hundred impressionable students. I do not think it is my place as a historian to preach my political views to them. But the closer I get to the present, particularly after the end of World War II, the more difficult I find it to resist the temptation. And since Watergate marks the beginning of my political consciousness, I draw the line there. Plus, for every lecture added after Watergate, I would have to cut major portions of the late nineteenth and/or early twentieth centuries. That trade-off does not appeal to me. I feel a much greater obligation to bring to life this earlier period, if for no other reason than most students believe that nothing much happened between the Civil War and World War I. Other instructors, of course, will surely want to make different trade-offs with regard to coverage or, perhaps, let a few big questions or specific themes drive their content choices. If, as a new teacher, you find these choices challenging, even intimidating, do not worry. It took me a few years to feel fully comfortable making these sorts of decisions. Follow your instincts, do the best you can, and do not be afraid to make changes from one semester to the next. As for all the other lectures listed in the schedule, do not let the generic titles fool you. They mask the importance of content and delivery (which are topics for the next chapter).

Important Note

The handouts used in this course are copyrighted. By "handouts," I mean all materials generated for this class, which include, but are not limited to, syllabi, exams, reading guides, and paper topics. Because these materials are copyrighted, you do not have the right to copy the handouts, unless I expressly grant permission. Also, *please do not record the lectures or take notes for any outside note-taking company without my permission.*

The "important note," I should confess, amounts to wishful thinking on my part. Its purpose is to discourage students from circulating the exams around campus for future use. In the big class, however, you cannot stop the flow of information no matter how hard you try. This necessitates altering your exams just enough to confuse potential cheaters every time you teach the course. On students' requests to record lectures, see Chapter 3.

Disabilities

The Americans with Disabilities Act (ADA) is a federal anti-discrimination statute that provides comprehensive civil rights protection for persons with disabilities. Among other things, this legislation requires that all students with disabilities be guaranteed a learning environment that provides for reasonable accommodation of their disabilities. If you believe you have a disability requiring an accommodation, please contact the Office of Support Services for Students with Disabilities in Room B-118 Cain Hall (555-1234).

Academic Integrity

"An Aggie does not lie, cheat, or steal, or tolerate those who do." You are expected to be aware of the Aggie Honor Code and the Honor Council Rules and Procedures, stated at http://www.tamu.edu/aggiehonor.

These mandatory statements are self-explanatory, but neither is wholly adequate. Even with the excellent support services we have at Texas A&M, students with special needs are often reluctant to identify themselves. Assuming the classroom reflects the general population, sixty of the three hundred students (one in five) will have some sort of physical or learning disability. You can make a big difference on the first day of class by simply inviting students who think they may need, say, extra time on an exam to contact you during office hours. All you will do, of course, is direct the student to the appropriate campus office—but that might very well have been a student who might not have gone otherwise. Far fewer students will consult the Aggie Honor Web site, as directed, to familiarize themselves with the rules and procedures concerning cheating and plagiarism. Nor does it help, in my humble opinion, to reduce something of this magnitude to an Aggie-ism. This is a matter better addressed face-to-face, on the first day of class, rather than in a line or two in the syllabus (see Chapter 3).

Guidelines for Writing Papers

[See Appendix A, pp. 103–4, for full details.]

This three-page supplement could just as well be distributed separately. But again, I include it with the syllabus to stress the importance of writing in HIST 106, even if it is not an English class. These guidelines are an integral part of the course, and the teaching assistants and I repeatedly stress their importance throughout the semester. The writing guidelines have evolved over the years from my personal experiences with first-year students, input from teaching assistants, and syllabi from courses I took as an undergraduate. (See Chapter 3 for a larger discussion about writing.)[10]

One Week to Go

With your syllabus ready, just a few practical matters remain before class begins. Ideally, you would want to familiarize yourself with all the various faculty and student services on campus, but that would be a Herculean task at a university as large as Texas A&M. Your best bet instead is to get to know—and know well—the staff, who are invariably the most well-informed people in the department. One way to start making a good impression is to submit your syllabus early for photocopying before the big rush comes at the end of the week. I would also recommend, if feasible, e-mailing your syllabus to your students a week or so in advance in addition to handing out hard copies on the first day of class—though again, do not expect them all to have read it, let alone digested it.

Be sure to familiarize yourself with whatever course-management system your university uses. Be sure also to take a peek at your lecture hall to familiarize yourself with the surroundings and its technological capabilities. You will probably need to establish an account to access the computer in the room. It is also crucial to meet with your teaching assistants (which I will cover in Chapter 3). Finally, it is an excellent idea to keep a class-by-class log over the course of the semester—just a few sentences at the end of each teaching day on what went well, what really needs to change, and what you might want to do differently the next time. You will find it invaluable when reviewing for the next semester.

Are you confident in your preparations? Probably not—at least not fully. But the day has come. It is on to the big show!

Notes

1. Lang, *On Course*, 202, 233.
2. Survey courses without discussion sections are especially numerous at Texas A&M. Because the state legislature mandates six units of U.S. history for all undergraduates, about five thousand students take HIST 105 or 106 every semester. That breaks down to twenty-five sections of two hundred students each—far too many for the department to staff each section with multiple discussion leaders. Instructors, in most cases, receive one graduate student grader.
3. Barbara Gross Davis, *Tools for Teaching* (San Francisco: Jossey-Bass, 1993), chap. 2, is especially good on the nuts and bolts of the course syllabus. For further discussion, see Todd Estes, "Constructing the Syllabus: Devising a Framework for Helping Students Learn to Think like Historians," *The History Teacher* 40 (February 2007): 183–202.
4. Lang, *On Course*, 3–4; Davis, *Tools for Teaching*, 15; and Linda B. Nilson, *Teaching at Its Best: A Research-Based Resource for College Instructors* (Bolton, Mass.: Anker, 2003), 27.

5. Lang, *On Course*, 90–92.
6. For further discussion, see Jean MacGregor et al., eds., *Strategies for Energizing Large Classes: From Small Groups to Learning Communities* (San Francisco: Jossey-Bass, 2000).
7. See also Davis, *Tools for Teaching*, 239–51; and Frank Heppner, *Teaching the Large College Class: A Guidebook for Instructors with Multitudes* (San Francisco: Jossey-Bass, 2007), 99–123.
8. On the pluses and minuses of taking attendance, see Lynda G. Cleveland, "That's Not a Large Class; It's a Small Town: How Do I Manage?"; Mary Deane Sorcinelli, "Promoting Civility in Large Classes"; and John R. Hoyle, "Making Large Classes Small through Creative Teaching," all in *Engaging Large Classes: Strategies and Techniques for College Faculty*, ed. Christine A. Stanley and M. Erin Porter (Bolton, Mass.: Anker, 2002), 16–27, 44–57, 186–99, respectively; and James M. Lang, *Life on the Tenure Track: Lessons from the First Year* (Baltimore: Johns Hopkins University Press, 2005), 121–22.
9. There are, of course, a wide range of academic calendars—not just semesters but quarters, winter terms, and summer sessions as well. Each requires its own set of adjustments.
10. While I do not assign published writing guides to my survey classes, a number of useful ones are available, including Jules Benjamin, *A Student's Guide to History*, Eleventh Edition (Boston: Bedford/St. Martin's, 2010); and Mary Lynn Rampolla, *A Pocket Guide to Writing in History*, Sixth Edition (Boston: Bedford/St. Martin's, 2010).

CHAPTER 2

In the Lecture Hall

"HOWDY!" says I to welcome them.

"HOWDY!" they respond in unison.

So begins every lecture in my large survey classes. Corny? Sure it is. Many of my colleagues in the history department would not be caught dead screaming "Howdy!" to their classes—and understandably so. "Howdy" is the "official" greeting at Texas A&M, a university so steeped in traditions that it is hard for "outsiders"—including, or perhaps even especially, faculty—to take them seriously. Just one example should suffice. Reveille is the official mascot of Texas A&M University. She is the highest-ranking member of the Corps of Cadets—a Five-Star General. She is also a dog. When Reveille dies, she is buried, next to her predecessors, facing the scoreboard at the football stadium so that she can always watch the Aggies outscore their opponent (which, alas, has not happened much of late). A few cadets have the high honor of taking care of Reveille, whom they address as "Miss Rev, ma'am." If she is sleeping on a cadet's bed, that cadet must sleep on the floor. If she is in class (yes, she comes to class) and barks while the professor is teaching, tradition holds that the class is to be immediately dismissed. I could go on, but I think you catch my drift.

Yet a thunderous exchange of "Howdy!" each day can really work to your advantage. From a practical standpoint, "Howdy!" gets the class ready to go almost instantaneously. Think about how difficult it is to get three hundred students, all chatting with their neighbors, to quiet down and turn their attention to you. With a simple "Hello" or "Good morning," I suspect it takes at least a couple of minutes before you can begin. They get such a kick out of "Howdy!" that they actually anticipate the moment, bellow it out on cue, and then are ready for me to start right then and there. The whole process takes about five seconds and has the added effect of getting them and me (yes, me, too) fired up! Admittedly, not every day starts with such gusto, as the midsemester doldrums inevitably set in. But all I have to do is scold them for a lackluster "Howdy," give them a second chance, and they blow the roof off the building.

I have learned over the years that a resounding greeting of "Howdy!" serves a much more important purpose than just getting the class going on time. It helps me establish a rapport with the class, which is absolutely crucial in a large introductory course for creating a productive teaching and learning environment. With three hundred students, it is simply not possible to develop a one-on-one relationship with all of them, except perhaps with the few who sit in the front row every day or with those who come to your office hours more than a couple of times. However, you can do some little things to help build a relationship of mutual trust and create an atmosphere of mutual respect — in essence, make it *feel* like they know you and you know them. For me, "Howdy" is one of them. (You may develop your own starting ritual that might fit your own style or university.) The "tips" section in the syllabus is another. There is no key moment or specific strategy, however, that by itself allows you to establish a meaningful rapport with your class. It takes a concerted effort all semester long, beginning with your first day in front of the big class.

The First Day of Class

Teaching guidebooks, almost without exception, place tremendous importance on the first day of class. "First impressions *do* count," says one. "During the first class meeting, the example you set . . . will create expectations that will last the entire semester." Says another, "Be a missionary [on the first day]. Explain why understanding your subject is essential for lifelong happiness and fulfillment; why without your course one cannot be an interesting or attractive person. Whet their appetites for what is to come." Recommendations abound for how to proceed. Start, of course, with a syllabus review, carefully explaining the nuts and bolts of the course. Stir students' intellectual curiosity about the subject matter of the course. Capture their interest. Build a sense of community. Plan an icebreaker or two to calm everyone's nerves. Start on time, and do not—whatever you do—dismiss them early. Above all else, be enthusiastic on the first day. "Enthusiasm is contagious. Your showing some of yours for the subject matter and the opportunity to teach it will motivate students' interest in learning it and inspire their respect for you as a scholar."[1]

This is all well and good—in the abstract, that is. In real life, however, it is not always that easy. What do you do if you are as nervous as I was on my very first day in front of the big class? I am sure that I had all kinds of activities planned to motivate my students that day. I do not recall with much clarity what actually happened when I returned to class from the bathroom, but I sincerely doubt much was accomplished—which surely made me feel all the more discouraged. So, another option—a perfectly good option, I think—is to walk in the first day with minimal plans and low expectations. Greet them, walk them through the syllabus, take a few questions, and yes, let them go early. They will love you for it. After all, they have three or four more first days of class that very day. You will have plenty of time to "whet their appetites" in the days and weeks ahead.[2]

This does not mean, however, that you should just blow off the first class meeting as a matter of course from that point on. To the contrary, try aiming a little higher on the first day of the next semester, and then a little higher after each time in subsequent semesters. You do not even have to abandon the always-reliable, always-comfortable syllabus review to accomplish this. There is no better way, for example, to demonstrate your enthusiasm than by entering the lecture hall with all the course books under your arm and laying them on the front table for everyone to see. Then, at the appropriate time, say a few words to, in effect, market the books to the class, as though you were on the Home Shopping Network:

> Our first book [holding it up like you are trying to sell them a George Foreman Grill] is a historical novel—a fictional account—written by Thomas Bell in 1941. The novel follows two generations of a Slavic immigrant family, starting with the family's migration from Austria-Hungary in 1880 to a small town in western Pennsylvania near Pittsburgh. The novel's title—*Out of This Furnace*—refers to the central role that steel plays in all phases of the family's life. It illustrates, in dramatic fashion, many of the main themes of the first

part of our course, including immigration, industrialization, and the rise of trade unionism, and it has a gripping plot full of sex and violence — you'll love it. [Three generations are actually covered in the novel; I assign the first half only.]

Then, we're going to read a book about Coney Island in New York City, which at the turn of the twentieth century was one of the first amusement parks in America, an amusement park not all that unlike the ones we go to today, such as Six Flags in Dallas and San Antonio. This book nicely complements my lecture on the rise of the modern city. What was it about city life, historian John Kasson asks, that made people feel the need for something like Coney Island? As you can tell, the book is full of great photographs [flip through the book to show them], but don't let that fool you. The book is more difficult to understand than it appears.

And so on, with the rest of the books. This would also be a good moment to emphasize the difference between a *novel* and a *book* (or monograph). For reasons that escape me, most high school graduates in America seem to believe that all books are novels (or at least can be called novels), even if the book is nonfiction.

Another way to get everyone's juices flowing on the first day is to ask all two or three hundred students to divide themselves into groups of five or six — right away, even before the syllabus review. This is especially useful in classes without discussion sections because (in my scheme) they will be breaking into small groups six more times over the course of the semester to discuss the books. It is, in other words, a dress rehearsal with no strings attached. Beware of the temptation, at this point, to have them read and discuss some sort of primary source or short essay, no matter how provocative you might think it is. There will be no exciting intellectual conversation — not much conversation of any kind — I can assure you. Instead, you will have three hundred eighteen- and nineteen-year-olds staring at each other in bewilderment and pondering the possibility of transferring into another section. If you are going to try an icebreaker like this, it needs to be engaging, but it also needs to be simple — something that allows everyone to participate with minimal effort.[3]

The way I proceed is to have the students introduce themselves to the rest of their group by telling each other their name, major, previous college history courses, reason for taking this course, and, to make things interesting, first historical memory. To get things going, I tell them my own—the JFK assassination—which always generates a few oohs and aahs. I might as well have said the Lincoln assassination, it often seems. One person in each group serves as secretary and records all the information to hand in at the end of class. For the next ten minutes, the bustle of the lecture hall does wonders for everyone's morale—theirs and mine. What a great feeling on the first day! It is not always a great feeling, however, to actually hear some of their first historical memories when I throw the discussion open to everyone for a few minutes. Monica Lewinsky? The Bush-Gore cliff-hanger? 9/11? I am telling you, these kids are getting younger every year! If you can withstand the shock to your system, this activity—an icebreaker, a community builder, and an appetite whetter all at once—works every time.

Another activity that I often add to the mix complements the "tips" section of the syllabus—in particular, the importance of reviewing their notes after each class. I draw a big circle on the blackboard, declare it to be a penny, and ask them to list the various features on both sides of the coin. "Abraham Lincoln." "The Lincoln Memorial." "The 'In God We Trust' motto." "The year it was minted." They usually do not get much farther than that. "OK," I continue. "Which way is Lincoln facing—from his perspective looking out at you?" A few of them shout "right" and a few others counter with "left," but no one sounds very confident. I then take a poll with a show of hands. Invariably, two-thirds of the class votes right, and one-third votes left. Occasionally a few say straight ahead, thinking it might be a trick question. The answer is left. "What does all this have to do with taking notes?" I ask them. When no one answers, I pause and then respond:

> We all handle lots of pennies all the time, yet only one-third of you knew which way Lincoln faces. Most of the winners were probably just guessing, I'm betting. But now, because you have interacted with the penny, you'll be able to impress your friends for weeks on end with your knowledge of it. The same holds true with your class notes. Interact with them on a regular basis—review and even annotate them while the lecture is still fresh in your mind—and you will be ready, when the time comes, to take the exams and do well.

In truth, I do not know how much, if any, this motivates them to review their notes, but it does liven things up a bit on the first day of class.

Discussing plagiarism will have just the opposite effect, but you should nonetheless save some time at the end of the first day to address this very serious issue. A required clause in the syllabus has its purpose, but there is no substitute for reading students the riot act face-to-face on this worst of academic sins. Change your demeanor so that they know you mean business. Move to the center of the stage and as close to them as possible. Alter the tone of your voice, speak a little slower, and try to look as many of them in the eye as possible. I try to keep it short and to the point:

> There are very few things that you can do in this class, and in college in general, that can get you into serious trouble. Plagiarism is one of them. When you try to pass off someone else's ideas, writings, paragraphs, sentences, or phrases as your own ideas, writings, paragraphs, sentences, or phrases, you are committing plagiarism — you are cheating. It doesn't matter where you steal from — books, magazines, journals, newspapers, or Web sites — it's all cheating. When writing the two papers for this class, the only source you will need, and the only source you should use, is the book on which you have chosen to write. Don't be tempted to even peek at the Internet for help — that in itself is cheating. Now, it is possible to cheat and get away with it sometimes. But the TAs and I are experts at identifying suspicious papers — it's really not that hard, actually. And believe me, if you found it on the Internet, we can find it on the Internet. When we catch you, we will turn the evidence over to the Honors Council, and these folks don't mess around. The penalties are severe, ranging from an F in the course to expulsion from the university. So when you get the urge to cheat, you might want to pause for a moment and ask yourself if it's worth it. It is always better — every time — to write a lousy paper and even take an F on it than to face the wrath of the Honors Council.

Unfortunately, there will be those in the class who cheat no matter what you say — many more than you will ever catch. No aspect of teaching is more frustrating or more unpleasant. (For more on cheating and how to respond, see Chapter 3.)

To end the first day on a less dour note, it is a good idea to revert to your pre-plagiarism demeanor for the last few minutes and encourage students, again, to make the most of your office hours. Freshmen, especially in big classes at large universities, can be greatly intimidated by the prospect of visiting even the kindest, most hospitable professor in his or her office. They may have to be invited many times before they consider taking the plunge. Do your best to make them feel welcome.[4]

Of far less importance, but sure to be on your mind nonetheless, is the dreaded question of what to wear on the first day, or any day, of class. Women have it much tougher than men on this issue, I readily admit. The only decision for men is this: tie or no tie. I wore a tie to class every day—without exception—as an assistant professor. On the day I received tenure, I looked into the closet and said to myself, "What the heck, no tie today." It became that much easier to say no tie the next day, and even easier the day after that. I have not worn a tie since. It is not just a personal decision, of course. Coat and tie are pretty much standard attire for academics across the South, but are reserved for formal occasions in the North. Probably no professor has worn a tie in California for decades. In my department, it is about 50/50. When choosing their clothing, women are more likely to ponder issues of authority, boundaries, and style, which are way beyond my area of expertise. My only advice would be to look around and see what everyone else is wearing, and then follow your instincts.[5]

In addition to developing a keen sense of fashion over the years, I have also discovered that what I most want to do on the first day of class is to hit the ground running. You might have noticed on the course schedule in the syllabus that I start the lecture on the Industrial Revolution at the end of the first day. I do this, in part, to begin preparing students for *Out of This Furnace*, and I need the extra twenty minutes or so to cover this vast topic in a timely manner. But the main reason I start lecturing right away is to begin to establish rapport with the students as soon as possible. What better way to get them excited about the course than to give them the impression that I cannot wait to get started? This is a gamble, I readily admit. And I do not recommend this approach for beginners who, as I stated earlier, might be better off sticking with the basics on the first day. But at this stage of my career, I am reasonably confident that I can review the syllabus, share a couple of icebreakers, and answer a few questions in the first half hour. (I also know that my teaching assistants will cover for me in the first discussion section later that week; see Chapter 3.) In the remaining twenty minutes, if I am to capture their attention and stimulate their intellectual curiosity, I need to be at the top of my game. But then, the same holds true for the rest of the semester.

The Fine Art of Lecturing

Don't plan a lecture for a full period. The average student's attention span is between ten and twenty minutes. After that, students have difficulty concentrating on the speaker.[6]

Social science research shows the adult attention span to be about 20 minutes at most and often much less.[7]

Student retention of material covered in the first 10 minutes of a lecture is about 70%; in the final 10 minutes of the lecture, retention is around 20%. . . . In a 50-minute lecture, students are attentive to the lecturer around 40% of the time.[8]

A lecture begins with a five-minute settling in period during which students are fairly attentive. This attentiveness extends another five to ten minutes, after which students become increasingly bored, restless, and confused. Focus and note-taking continue to drop — some students effectively fall asleep — until the last several minutes of the period when they revive in anticipation of the end of the class.[9]

Many more such statements can be found where these came from. Indeed, it would be difficult to find even a single major teaching guidebook that claims otherwise. The experts, it seems, have spoken.

Balderdash! (The publisher will not let me use the other, preferable, b-word.)

Talk about a negative self-fulfilling prophecy! The experts, for many years now, have bashed the lecture with such glee, citing themselves over and over again, that its demise, in the literature of higher education, appears all but inevitable.[10] If you allow yourself to buy into the twenty-minute attention span theory, it will become true—that much is certain. This is not to say that holding students' attention in the large lecture hall is easy—far from it. It is especially difficult for large introductory surveys, where most of the students have enrolled not because of their love of history, but because the university (or the state, in the case of Texas) requires them to take the course. And for all I know, short attention spans really are the norm for introductory courses in chemistry or economics. But this, my friends, is *history*, and you are a *historian*. You have great material! Of course you can plan a lecture that will capture students' attention for fifty or even seventy-five minutes—with hard work and dedication, that is. Please, do not give up the ship before you have even tried to set sail. Instead, let us launch a self-fulfilling prophecy of our own—a *positive* self-fulfilling prophecy.

How can I be so sure, you might ask. An expressive, enthusiastic instructor may be able to ignite students' interest in the material, but what about those of us who are, by nature, more quiet and reserved? Is there not something to the notion that good lecturers are born and not made? In a word, no. Good lecturers may make it look easy, even "natural," but they will be the first to tell you that good old-fashioned hard work has no substitute for success in the classroom. There is no one right way to lecture, and no one right personality to be an effective lecturer. I have no data, per se, to prove this. But I do have my observations, usually from the back row of the lecture hall, of dozens of instructors—graduate student lecturers, adjuncts, new faculty, and more seasoned teachers as well. Sketches of several of them, drawn from my notes, not only should be instructive in following the learn-by-example approach of this book, but also should help put to rest the notion that the lecture, as a teaching method, has limited value. Reports of its death are premature.

No one made it look more "natural" than Kale, one of the many adjuncts I have observed over the years. I am not in the habit of giving excessive praise, but Kale was sensational in the lecture hall, even with his limited experience. In my observations of his teaching, he was comfortable and, indeed, held command in class. He seemed utterly at ease with students, welcomed their questions, and enjoyed discussions with them in and out of the classroom. Perhaps most important, Kale knew how to *motivate* students—no easy task, particularly in survey courses full of eighteen- and nineteen-year-olds who would rather have been just about anywhere else. His lecture was well prepared; was presented with humor, enthusiasm, and down-to-earth language; employed insights from "the classics" as well as cutting-edge scholarship; and used Power-Point skillfully (but judiciously). What really made Kale stand out, however, was his incredible energy. In an oddly shaped auditorium that was more wide than it was deep, Kale paced furiously from one end of the stage to the other as though to keep all 245 students *physically* involved. Every ten minutes or so, he stopped (his lecture, not his pacing) to fire questions into the crowd. Students—even those in the back row—actually competed with one another for a chance to respond. I found it exhausting just to watch, but Kale kept going for a full hour and fifteen minutes—making an absolute mockery of the twenty-minute attention span theory.

While Kale's persona in the lecture hall matched his overall out-going, dynamic personality, Scott, a graduate student lecturer, was much more of a Dr. Jekyll and Mr. Hyde. He was painfully, perhaps even pathologically, shy—so much so that he literally could not look you in the eye when conversing, which he avoided as much as possible. We worried about him leading discussion sections, and in truth, he was not very good at it, for just being in the room with all those kids made him intensely nervous. So, it was with great trepi-dation that I went to observe him lecture during his first semester in the classroom. Imagine my surprise when, from the moment class started, he took off like a house afire! He had full command of the subject—the New Deal, a very difficult lecture to draft and deliver. I never have figured out how to make all those alphabet agencies interesting. Scott spoke clearly, engagingly, and with con-siderable passion, and held their attention every bit as much as Kale (and in the same odd auditorium). And for good measure, he told a few jokes—good ones, at that! He even had a shtick going, holding a bottle of Coca-Cola (or was it Dr Pepper?) the whole time, though never drinking from it, not unlike Groucho Marx and his ever-present cigar. What a ham! Never before or since have I seen such a split personality. It just goes to show you that while the lecture is a special form of communication, it does not require a special type of lecturer.

Like Kale and Scott, Warren, one of our new assistant pro-fessors, performed at a level well beyond his experience when I observed his lecture. His stage presence was simply captivating:

He spoke with a loud, clear voice and managed to vary his delivery to keep students' attention; he used concrete, simple, and colorful language, even when explaining complex issues; he unleashed the power of his arms and hands to emphasize his main points, including pounding his fist on the lectern or in his palm a few times; and he rarely, if ever, consulted his lecture notes. He had his audience, well, in the palm of his hand. Warren was all the more impressive because he pitched his lecture (on twentieth-century international relations) at a very high level—much higher than either Kale or Scott. But it did not seem to matter. Students took notes like crazy and asked questions—lots of questions—not only during the lecture, but after at the podium, on the way back to his office, and even in his office for some time afterward. He looked like the Pied Piper walking across campus. Warren's only problem was that he talked very fast, prompting one brave student to ask him, politely, to please slow down. Warren tried his best to accommodate the request, but was back at full throttle within a couple of minutes. I have yet to observe anyone who could noticeably change the pace—slow down or speed up—at which they lecture. The only thing fast talkers can do, it seems to me, is to force themselves to pause every few minutes to allow students to catch up. From what I could tell, no one in Warren's class seemed too upset. He challenged his students in multiple ways, and they responded in impressive fashion. He *inspired* them.

Neither Kale, Scott, nor Warren employed PowerPoint very much, other than to put up a brief outline of the lecture at the outset or display a map or two. Craig, a graduate student lecturer, relied on it heavily, in contrast. He kept a rolling outline throughout his lecture, replacing one densely worded slide with another every ten minutes or so. This has become a very common strategy of late among new lecturers, in particular. PowerPoint has become so popular, so ubiquitous in lecture halls that new teachers think they *must* use it and that its value as a teaching tool is beyond dispute. Craig's intent with PowerPoint was admirable: He wanted to emphasize the main points of the lecture as well as to help his students keep their focus. From my perspective in the back of the room, however, his approach with PowerPoint was largely counterproductive. When a new slide appeared, every student seemed to respond in exactly the same way: They copied all the bullet points word for word in their notebooks—a task that took several minutes. While they were writing, however, they all but tuned out Craig's lecture. And in the few minutes after they finished copying the text and before the next slide, they took nary a single note. It was as though they had all been programmed by some evil villain on *Batman* to act against their best interests. Craig could have just e-mailed them the slides, canceled the lecture, and gotten the same result.

Can PowerPoint or some other technology be put to better use in the lecture hall? Of course. But I've observed that most instructors share Craig's perception: They think they are enhancing their lectures, but students' reactions suggest otherwise. Take Ernie, for example, a prominent historian at another university. Ernie is very serious about his teaching. He took an effective, no-nonsense approach to his survey class, prepared his lecture carefully, and employed PowerPoint extensively. Maps, photographs, graphs, charts—you name it, he used it, one slide after another. But even though much thought went into the presentation, I found myself distracted at least as often as I found myself engaged. As I looked at each slide, I invariably turned my focus away from Ernie and, in the process, missed several of his main points. Maybe others multitask better than I do, I thought. But as I looked around the room, students everywhere seemed just as fixated on the screen as I had been, much to their detriment as well. Unwittingly, Ernie had created a learning environment in which he was competing with PowerPoint for his students' attention.

Technology works much better, it has always seemed to me, when used sparingly or apart from the lecture itself. Laura, a colleague of Ernie's, demonstrated this to near perfection, I thought, in her lecture on the gay rights movement in San Francisco. Rather than using a rolling outline, she arrived ten minutes before class started to put a full outline on the screen for students to note in advance. She showed just a couple of additional PowerPoint slides, each time analyzing the image carefully and stimulating a few questions. Then, in the last twenty-five minutes of the period, she showed a video of Harvey Milk's life that ended with the chilling scene of a young, bewildered Dianne Feinstein, surrounded by reporters and microphones, announcing the assassinations of Supervisor Milk and Mayor George Moscone on November 27, 1978. The video conveyed the *emotion* of the gay rights movement in a way that no lecture could have captured.

A few additional (and, in some cases, more lighthearted) observations:

Low-Tech Magic To teach his students the fine points of historical analysis, Steven, a community college teacher, projected high-tech PowerPoint and Internet images of actual documents on the low-tech whiteboard in his classroom. This allowed him to underline important sentences and circle key phrases with a dry-erase marker for all the students to see. Brilliant!

Whiteboard Crisis What do you do when the [expletive] professor in the period before yours writes all over the whiteboard with a *permanent* marker? Kate, my teaching assistant, instructed me to simply draw like a two-year-old, up and down and all around, over the "permanent" scribbles with a dry-erase marker, and then just erase the board. Poof! It all disappeared like magic. (The solvent in dry-erase markers will dissolve most permanent marker inks.)

Olé! Larry, in his Latin American Studies introductory survey course at a large and prestigious public university, arrived ten minutes early to class and played loud salsa music to fire up his students (and himself, I presume). The question was whether he could sustain that level of energy for the full fifty minutes. But Larry, in a powerful lecture on the Cuban and Chilean revolutions, pulled it off—not by yelling and screaming and jumping up on the table, but with a relaxed, conversational style all his own.

The Rifleman When he paused to ask questions, Calvin, an adjunct lecturer, extended his two arms out together, pointed them like a rifle, and scanned the entire lecture hall as though placing his students under arrest. Unorthodox, but very effective, as evidenced by the rate at which students shot questions back at him.

Focused Carrie organized her entire course, "Introduction to European History," around one core question: How is it that the same continent, and sometimes even the same people, could give rise to the notions of terror and human rights? She also prohibited computers of any kind in the classroom to prevent students from multitasking, going on Facebook, etc. Both strategies seemed to keep her students exceptionally focused in the lecture hall; they took notes as though their lives depended on it. Did they even know, I wondered, that their professor is blind? Or that one out of five faculty members (assuming they reflect the population as a whole) has a disability?[11]

The Slide of a Hand A former professor of mine, who taught the big survey course as well as anyone I have seen, began every class with his left hand resting on his lower back, the tips of his fingers just inside his trousers. As he proceeded with his lecture, his hand gradually slid farther and farther down until by the end of the period he was wrist-deep in trouble—I kid you not. The TAs in the back row (myself included) could barely contain themselves, but the professor never missed a beat.

Video Madness Perhaps my professor should have watched himself on videotape. At least, that is what all the various teaching guidebooks prescribe. "Often we must actually see our good behaviors in order to exploit them and see our undesirable behaviors in order to correct them," states one in typical fashion.[12] If viewing a videotape of yourself sounds appealing to you, then by all means do not hesitate. Teaching centers on campuses across the country will be pleased to assist you. I for one, however, could not do it. If I were to watch myself live, in action, I am not sure if I could ever get up there again. It would be worse—way worse—than hearing myself on a tape recorder or phone answering machine. Like my professor with the sliding hand, and perhaps to my detriment as well, I would just as soon not know.

In fact, I seem to violate quite a bit of the standard prescriptive advice for delivering effective lectures. It is not that I am some sort of radical out to defy the conventional wisdom of the teaching guidebooks. (I was not even aware of the conventional wisdom, quite frankly, before I began this book.) This is simply my style, for lack of a better word, as it has evolved over the years, as I have come to know the students, lecture halls, material, and most important, myself as a teacher.

A few more glaring violations of mine:

"Avoid lecturing verbatim from a script."[13] Actually, I write out all my lectures, word for word, print them out in an easy-to-see format (14-point font, double-spaced), and have the script, in its entirety, on the podium, right in front of me. The advantages are real and numerous. Many of the lectures I have observed, even some of the very good ones, were not self-contained. The instruc-

tor merely picked up where he/she left off the previous period, and stopped whenever the time ran out, in a continuous timeline fashion. My lectures, in contrast, are designed to be more like chapters in a book, in that each has its own structure, central theme, supporting evidence, and direct links to previous and future topics. Writing them out, therefore, helps me to decide exactly what I need to cover, how to organize my thoughts in meaningful sequence, how to get the wording of difficult explanations exactly the way I want it, and how to get the timing right as well. I know, from past experience, that eleven pages, give or take half a page, fills a fifty-minute period perfectly for me, with a few minutes left over for questions.

This is substantially less time than the standard estimate of two minutes a page for delivering a conference paper (i.e., ten pages for a twenty-minute presentation). But a lecture is not a conference paper, of course. Though I write out the lecture, I do so for the ear, not the eye. Thus, I construct short, straightforward sentences; I use simple, even informal, words and phrases, including personal pronouns, contractions, idioms, and other forms of plain-talking language; I make the same transitions that are emphasized in the lecture outlines; and I underline, with a blue pen, the key concepts and phrases so that I will be sure not to forget them. Though the approach is different with a lecture than a written essay, the objectives are the same: clarity of expression, economy of words, and clear, logical organization. With my written work, I strive to develop a distinct rhythm from sentence to sentence, paragraph to paragraph. With my lectures, I seek to establish a strong cadence.

Just because I write out my lectures does not mean I give them with my head down, buried in the script (as the guidebooks invariably imply). I know my lectures very well, but I do not read, memorize, or rehearse them. I *deliver* them. With the content, language, structure, and narrative flow already worked out in my mind, I can then give the presentation itself, knowing that I have mastered the material. That gives me the confidence to *engage* my large audience—to perform with spontaneity, animation, expressiveness, and flexibility, as well as to maintain eye contact and a sense of dialogue and direct engagement. This approach also helps me, I think, avoid the annoying speech mannerisms—"you know," "like," "uhhhh," "okay"—that often accompany more extemporaneous deliveries. And I can also concentrate on varying the pace, volume, and emotion at which I speak, to lend emphasis to my main points. Separating the brain work of the lecture from the performance itself, therefore, allows me to communicate to the full extent of my ability with the three hundred students before me.

A picture is worth a thousand words. This adage (supposedly from an old Chinese proverb) has never been more relevant than in the current digital age. With every passing day, it seems, pictures (images, in twenty-first-century parlance) are becoming even more vital than words in the myriad of ways in which we communicate. Maybe so, but not in my classroom. From my critiques of Craig's and Ernie's lectures, you may have already pegged me as some sort of technophobe. And, as if to confirm that, a student recently wrote on the back of a course evaluation form, "Join the 21st century, Vaught!" But I consciously and steadfastly refuse. At the risk of sounding stuck all the way back in the nineteenth century, I rely on the written word and the spoken word, period. I will say it again—college students do not read nearly enough today, nor do they listen particularly well. They *prefer* to look at images and, as the students in Craig's and Ernie's classes revealed, will stare at them automatically, without pause for concern, because that has become their default option. I offer them no temptation, therefore. No PowerPoint. No WebCT. No overhead projector. No TV monitors. No "pictures" of any kind, except the lecture outline that I write on the blackboard before class. I might also take a piece of chalk and sketch a map, on occasion.

Blackboard? Chalk? If you are baffled, imagine what the students are thinking when they see me writing on the blackboard every day. (Well, I guess the quote in the previous paragraph gives you some indication.) Why, you may well be asking, do I not at least display the outline with PowerPoint or an overhead projector to save myself the time and effort of writing it on the board? In my mind, the lecture outline has two purposes. It lets students know in advance what to expect that day and, even more important, it helps them keep their focus all the way through the lecture. Thus, they need to copy it down, preferably before class starts, and to refer to it, as needed. They do not need to stare at it for minutes on end, however. But I guarantee you that is what they do when the outline is projected up on a big screen, where it is much more obtrusive than on the blackboard. Pardon my ego, but I want their attention on *me* for the full fifty minutes. Plus, I believe it is to my advantage to arrive at least ten minutes early and leave a few minutes late (to erase the board), as it gives students the chance to ask me questions or to just interact with me on an informal basis. I am not trying to rid all classrooms of technology or convert you into a Luddite. I ask merely that you take note of the method to my madness and use technology mindfully. I have seen too many young instructors seduced by it, at considerable cost to the quality of their teaching.[14]

"Move out into the seats to speak to the back of the room; move to different sides of the room to speak to the corners; move in front of individual desks and speak for a minute or two to one person, as if you and she were standing on the quad exchanging ideas."[15] I am pretty much a podium hugger, actually. I will stray three or four steps away, but that is it. I feel more in control near the podium and, to be blatantly honest, do not want to get too far away from my script. Knowing it is there, and knowing that I can refer to it in a pinch, gives me a high level of comfort that, in turn, makes the whole lecture go that much more smoothly. And on days when, for whatever reason, the lecture may not be going very well, the security of the script on the podium becomes all the more important to me. I admire Kalc and Warren for their ability to stroll back and forth across the stage so effortlessly. But when I tried it years ago, I simply was not very good at it, and my lectures suffered as a result. The moral of the story: Play to your own natural and acquired strengths, not to someone else's.

The simplicity of that statement masks its profoundness. I have seen many new and even more seasoned instructors get themselves into trouble by trying to be someone or something they are not. Students can spot such behavior a mile away. A study from 1987 (and still widely cited) determined the four characteristics that students most value in their professors who teach large classes: competency ("knows what he's talking about," as they often write on evaluations); concern for students (friendly, caring, and available); high energy and enthusiasm; and speaking ability (easy to understand and interesting).[16] These were all based on students' perceptions, of course. They do not know, for example, if the professor really knows what he or she is talking about or if the professor really has concern for them. But perception is crucial in a large class because you cannot possibly get to know all of the students, nor they you. You can, however, create an atmosphere—a rapport, to use that term again—that makes them feel less anonymous or isolated, and you do this by coming across as genuine, assertive, and attentive. In the large lecture hall, this requires a special form of communication. Your delivery and manner set the tone for the whole course and, in the process, immeasurably influence your students' ability to learn in an environment where opportunities for personal attention are limited.

Lecture Content

If delivery and manner set the tone for the course, the content of your lectures provides the foundation. If you look at the course schedule in either my 105 or 106 syllabus (see Appendix A), the lecture topics will no doubt seem very familiar. In most survey courses (U.S. history, in particular, perhaps), few will stray too far from the standard sequence. (The same holds true for chapter titles in textbooks.) How each lecturer chooses to handle each topic, however, varies widely, reflecting the individual's interests, preferences, and philosophy. Some lecturers, for example, have students rely on the assigned textbook for the historical narrative and then focus their lectures on more specific, complementary topics. Others, myself included, do just the opposite; they tell the story themselves and select readings that provide greater depth on selected issues. It is difficult, therefore, to make specific recommendations with regard to content without descending into the details of one approach while excluding the other. Once again, learning by example will have to suffice. I will try to give you an idea of what I do and let you be the judge.

What *do* I do? The simple answer is that I introduce the main themes, events, and personalities of American history. But *main* is such a subjective term. How do I decide? Do I have an ideological ax to grind of one kind or another? No, not really. I am, by nature, a centrist. But I am driven by two essential goals—one intellectual, the other more practical. History, I believe, is more than just "general education"; it is the quintessential liberal art. I want students—especially freshmen—to leave my classes thinking *differently* about themselves and the world than when they began. This can take the form of a mastery of the subject matter, a newfound introspection and questioning of their cultural assumptions, or even just a moment during the course, during a lecture, or while reading a book, that captures their imagination. From a more practical standpoint, I want students to end up genuinely excited about history and develop an active engagement with the subject. No matter what their major or future profession may be, the ability to think independently, use good judgment, and derive pleasure from learning will be more useful to them in the long run than any job-specific training.

These rather lofty ambitions compel me, first of all, to aim high when putting together my lectures. I do not think my lectures would be any different whether I gave them to large lecture halls in Seattle, Boston, or College Station, Texas. On the other hand, I remind myself repeatedly, these are eighteen- and nineteen-year-olds, who are not always inspired to learn the material. There is a fine line, in other words, between having high expectations and pitching the content over their heads. My solution is to choose a variety of sophisticated subjects—such as the labor movement (going back to the 1830s), the advent of "high society" in American cities at the turn of the twentieth century, the rise and fall of New Deal liberalism, or feminism—but make them accessible with simple, everyday language and straightforward explanations. Students get an especially heavy dose of slavery in the first half of the survey, including two books to read, parts of several lectures, and an entire fifty minutes on life in the slave quarters. I include that lecture not only because it is essential to my ongoing narrative, but because students find it provocative. Here is how it starts (see the lecture outline in Appendix C):

> It is very difficult for us to imagine what it must have been like to have been a slave in the Antebellum South. As we saw last time, slaves lived and worked under brutal conditions—far worse than for those of even the worst paid industrial worker in the North—and without any of the freedoms contemporary white Americans took for granted. So it's almost impossible not to think of them only as victims—victims of an oppressive labor system over which they had no control.
>
> But it would be shortsighted of us to perceive slaves simply as victims. They actually had a tremendous impact on American history. In the early decades of the new republic, conflict among whites over slavery was not that big of a deal. To slave owners, of course, there was no conflict whatsoever. In the South, the

centrality of slave labor was obvious. Southern whites' whole way of life depended on the efforts of enslaved black workers. In the North, a growing number disapproved of slavery on moral principle, yet still deemed it a matter of importance primarily to the South — it was a southern matter.

How was it, then, that slavery became such a big deal to northerners by the 1850s? Why, to put it another way, did northerners come to regard the institution of slavery so strongly and with such passion that they would eventually put their lives on the line to abolish it? This is one of the biggest questions — perhaps the biggest question of all — in American history, so we're going to take today and at least three additional class periods to consider it.

Now, many of you are probably familiar with the way in which slavery became a political issue in the 1840s and '50s — with events like the Wilmot Proviso, the Compromise of 1850, and the like. But to fully understand the origins of the Civil War, the Civil War itself, and the Reconstruction period that followed, we have to first understand things from the slaves' perspective. Above all else, it was the beliefs and actions of the African Americans themselves that compelled white society in the North to reexamine its values and assumptions. Slaves refused to accept their lot passively. At times, slaves turned to collective force and attempted against all odds to rise in revolt against their masters. Far more often, however, they resisted the burdens and humiliations of slavery the only way they could — by covertly frustrating their owners and by setting limits on their power. Where did slaves get the wherewithal to accomplish all this? In their own slave quarter right on the plantation. So that's where we will start today. . . .

I also try to impress upon students that historians often differ dramatically in their interpretations of key events. This does not mean, however, that I load them down with historiography or constant references to "historians," named or otherwise. That would surely bore them (and me) to death. But I will, on occasion, give them alternate interpretations, as I do at the end of "The Road to Rebellion, 1763–1775" (see lecture outline in Appendix C):

Now, just how did all this come about? Why did this sequence of events culminate in a massive armed struggle for independence that no one had foreseen, much less desired, only a dozen years before? And who, when it was all said and done, was responsible?

So far, I've put a pretty strong pro-colonist twist on things. The colonists were merely trying to defend their political and constitutional rights as British citizens — rights they had exercised for over 150 years. Rather than acknowledging those rights, the British tried to enforce Parliamentary supremacy and, in the process, made one bad decision after another that ultimately pushed the colonists into a position they never wanted to be in. In this view, the colonists were reluctant revolutionaries trying simply to preserve their rights as British citizens.

But were the colonists' motives based solely on preserving their liberty? No, say most British historians. Indeed, if seen from a British perspective, these events add up to something quite different. The key question asked by British historians is this: If the colonists' motives were based solely on preserving their liberty, then why did they keep changing their argument as events unfolded? In the controversy over the Stamp Tax, the colonists argued that Britain could only tax on an "external" rather than an "internal" basis. But the Townshend duties on lead, paper, paint, tea, and glass were external duties, so the colonists said that Parliament could not tax at all; it could only regulate trade. But when the Tea Act — an act solely for regulating trade — was implemented, the colonists whined again and said that Parliament could legislate, but not on issues that could even be construed as taxes. But again, the colonists cried foul when the Coercive Acts were passed, even though taxation was not an issue.

So what should we conclude from this line of reasoning? The colonists did not mean "no taxation without representation"; they meant no taxation period. All their arguments were simply constitutional smoke screens for what they were really interested in, and that was their own pocketbooks. At a time when the British really needed the colonists most to help pay the war debt, the colonists, like a bunch of ungrateful babies, deserted them. We should blame the colonists for the whole mess; it never would have happened but for their selfish, economic concerns.

Now, we've only scratched the surface in terms of the number of explanations offered for the American Revolution. The Gross book that you are now reading adds yet another perspective — that

of the residents of Concord, Massachusetts — which I shall leave
for you to ponder [Robert Gross, *The Minutemen and Their World*].
Then, on Friday, we'll look at three more possibilities, embodied
in how three specific individuals — George Hewes, Abigail Adams,
and Thomas Paine — experienced the Revolutionary era.

To offer one last example of what I do (and do not do), I turn
to my lecture on the Constitution. Here is how it begins (see the
lecture outline in Appendix C):

Has anyone seen the original, hand-written Constitution in Wash-
ington, D.C.? It's displayed in a bulletproof case in the Rotunda of
the National Archives Building. At night, the case descends into
a vault behind five-ton doors that are designed to withstand a
nuclear explosion. So, while you and I may go to sleep one night
and get obliterated in a nuclear war, the Constitution will be safe.

Doesn't this sound just a little bit overboard? Or, does this tell
us something about how Americans regard the Constitution? We
have no monarchy and no national religion. Some would say that
the Constitution is a substitute — and even that the "founding
fathers" wrote it under divine guidance.

Today, we're going to take the Constitution off its pedestal
and examine it in historical context. If you take away anything
at all from this class, understand that the founding fathers were
human beings and that the Constitution is a human document.
The Constitutional Convention was above all else a political event,
and the founding fathers were above all else seasoned politicians
with a myriad of conflicting agendas to push. So, anytime you hear
a politician or media pundit begin a sentence with, "The founding
fathers believed in . . . ," beware that they are probably feeding you
a line of bull. If anything, taking the Constitution off its pedestal
for a few minutes should give you an even greater appreciation for
this remarkable document.

From the moment it was created in 1787, the Constitution was
a complex and controversial document. It was written in a time
of crisis, and it embodied the values and interests of men with a
personal stake in its outcome. Fifty-five delegates attended the
Philadelphia Convention that began in May. They represented
every state except Rhode Island, whose legislature opposed any
increase in central authority. Almost all of them were seasoned

politicians, many of whom had been involved in American politics since the Stamp Act. They were all, it should be noted, from the upper crust of American society — merchants, lawyers, and slave-owning planters — with the exception of one yeoman farmer. And they were all nationalists — that is, they were committed to the creation of a central government that, as Alexander Hamilton put it, would protect the republic from "the imprudence of democracy" then engulfing the country.

The phrase "the imprudence of democracy" sounds a lot different than "life, liberty, and the pursuit of happiness" and other majestic phrases that had rolled off Jefferson's tongue in the Declaration of Independence. And indeed, the tone of these leading statesmen was considerably more sobering in 1787 than it had been in 1776. It was one thing to create a revolutionary manifesto, they had found out, but quite another to actively construct a working government that could somehow deal with inflation, debt, taxes, farmer rebellions, and the other problems that we looked at last time. . . .

Constitutional scholars will recognize immediately that the content of my lecture hardly reflects state-of-the-art scholarship. Much of it, in fact, draws from an article first published in 1961, whose central theme has long since been discredited for making Madison, Hamilton, et al. appear too much like twentieth-century political reformers.[17] For HIST 105, however, that does not bother me. I am far less interested in giving students cutting-edge interpretations than I am in giving them provocative interpretations. The notion that the Constitution was not the product of some abstract, philosophical commitment among the convention delegates, however much my source may have exaggerated it, not only meets my standard for intrigue but also gives students something to think about beyond what they hear on television.

It is no accident that the three excerpts I chose came from the first half of the U.S. survey, rather than the second. Even though my own research is centered more in the modern era, I find that I teach the early period better. Most of HIST 106 comes much easier for me, but in a way that makes me less self-critical and less concerned about how I come across. Yet no matter how many times I have taught HIST 105, I end up having to explain it to myself all over again, which results, I think, in clearer, more thoughtful explanations in the classroom. Remember, the idea is to *engage* students, not to show them how smart you are.

Maintaining Order

Quiz Question You have a great lecture prepared; you are delivering it with vim and vigor; and then, with twenty minutes still to go, two students suddenly stand up, climb over several others in the row in making their way to the aisle, and walk out of the lecture hall, letting the door bang behind them. What should you do?

    A. Scream at them to sit down as soon as they stand up.
    B. Add a section to your syllabus on the do's and don'ts of classroom behavior.
    C. Nothing. Ignore them.
    D. All the above.

    Answer: *d*, all the above.

Which is to say, I have responded in all three ways (and numerous others as well) at one time or another, depending on my mood and the level of commotion caused by the rude students. As for the subject of my quiz question, I could have substituted (for early leavers) late arrivers, newspaper readers, talkers and gigglers, sleepers, note passers, chronic clock checkers, texters and video game players, and the dreaded cell-phone-leaver-oners—all those good folks who made my first semester in the big classroom so memorable. How does one manage student behavior effectively in such a large class? There are two cut-and-dried methods, at opposite extremes, for maintaining order: the Attila the Hun approach and the three wise monkeys approach.[18]

Professor Hun includes a lengthy section on "classroom behavior" in his syllabus where, with words in capital letters and italics, he lays down the law, explicitly prohibiting latecomers, early goers, newspapers, cell phones, laptop computers—anything he finds disruptive to his classroom. On the first day of class, Dr. Hun reads this section aloud in his most authoritative voice and then asks for questions, knowing that the long period of silence that is sure to follow will bring home his point all the more. Should a student break one of the sacred rules at any point in the semester, Dr. Hun will not hesitate to inflict embarrassment and humiliation for all to see. A few examples: Dr. Hun thinks nothing of leaving the podium, right in the middle of his lecture, to march all the way to the back of the auditorium to snatch the newspaper out of a student's hands; he delights in actually answering a student's ringing cell phone and telling the caller that her friend is in class and cannot be disturbed; he routinely locks the doors of the lecture hall at the top of the hour to keep anyone from coming or going during class time; and he kicks students out of class at the drop of a hat for talking, passing notes, and any other action he deems disorderly. Needless to say, students understand that Professor Hun means business. They regard him as a policeman or, worse, a prison guard, and learn very quickly to sit still and let him rule the class with an iron fist.

Professor Monk, in contrast, says to himself, "See no evil, hear no evil, speak no evil," when classroom disruptions occur. He notices when students arrive late or leave early, but he takes no action. He notices when students are reading the newspaper or whispering to one another, but he prefers to ignore them rather than make a scene in the middle of class. He notices when a cell phone rings, but he lectures right through it. And he notices when students start putting away their notebooks and putting on their jackets five minutes before the end of the period, but again he chooses to look the other way. Dr. Monk tells himself that a relaxed atmosphere is more important to him than strict adherence to a set of behavioral rules. But a few weeks later, when a student walks into the lecture hall ten minutes late, causing little if any commotion, Dr. Monk blows up, letting out a semester's worth of frustration on one individual. He finds the student after class to apologize, but everyone else is left wondering what had happened.

Most of us, I think it is safe to say, have a classroom management style that leans toward either Dr. Hun or Dr. Monk, and most of us probably see a little bit of both of the good professors in ourselves. This has certainly been the case for me. On two occasions that come to mind, I completely lost it, just like Dr. Monk. One came during a brief discussion when a student made an overtly homophobic remark with a smart-ass tone that expressed how pleased he was with himself. Without thinking or hesitating, I told him—loudly—to get the hell out of the classroom and never come back. I then gave the other 299 students a short (and different sort of) lecture explaining that I simply do not tolerate that kind of behavior in my class. The second occasion stemmed from my own pent-up frustration. For some time, off and on for several weeks, two students in the back of the room had been yakking away with each other, even when I made a point to stare right at them as I was lecturing. Perhaps it is the sheer physical space of the lecture hall that gives some students the impression that they are invisible. Like Dr. Monk, I let their inappropriate behavior continue too long without addressing it until one day—boom!—I snapped, screamed at them, and threw them out of the class. I must say, however, that I had no further such problems that semester from the remaining students.

Even though part of me wants to be more like Professor Hun, it is just not my nature to constantly berate students. I have, however, developed a few strategies over the years to avoid the pitfalls of Professor Monk's passive-aggressive approach. In a large lecture hall of three hundred students, disruptions are going to occur that you just have to let go. On any given day, a small percentage of students will arrive late for any number of reasons, will have to get up in the middle of your lecture to use the bathroom, and will have to leave early to get somewhere else across campus. This has nothing to do with you or the quality of your teaching. Similarly, do not take it personally if someone is staring off into space, checking the clock, yawning, or even reading the dreaded newspaper. If a cell phone rings, you might want to stare down the culprit or squirm noticeably until he or she turns it off. That is usually enough to get the point across, until another one rings later on, which invariably will happen (it might even be yours!). Of course, if any of these disruptions get out of hand, you have to address them. But keep in mind that you can use your mean, loud voice only so many times before it loses its impact. I reserve it only for the most serious of matters, such as for explaining plagiarism or denouncing totally inappropriate behavior. You have to pick your spots.

It is even more important, it seems to me, to set the tone with your own behavior. For me, that means keeping a positive attitude toward the vast majority of the students who are well behaved, rather than being negative toward the few who are not. It bears repeating that, as with attendance, classroom behavior has improved in my big classes over the years first and foremost because I have improved over the years. The best way to minimize disruption is to command students' attention. Start on time every time, institute a starting ritual (like "Howdy!"), and deliver knock-out lectures, and you will create an atmosphere conducive to positive, respectful behavior much more effectively than by screaming at them all the time. Students are also likely to be more attentive if their grade depends on it, as in my survey courses, where 60 percent of the exams come directly from the lectures and nowhere else. If they would rather surf the Internet than take notes, it will cost them in my class. This approach, I have found, works better for me over the long haul than Dr. Hun's (and Carrie's) practice of outlawing laptops. Nor does it hurt to have a bit of fun with them from time to time. To avoid the inevitable commotion that comes during the final minutes of class, for example, I let them go five minutes early once every three weeks or so—before they get the urge to squirm and shuffle—but on the condition that they *owe* me those minutes (in case I need a couple of extra ones somewhere down the line) and that they must sit still through the end of every class until I am done. This approach—implemented with much drama and humor, of course—turns a problem into a game. It also gives me yet another way to establish and maintain a meaningful rapport with the big class.

Strategies for controlling the big class, when it is all said and done, depend on the personalities and goals of the instructor and often vary from semester to semester, even from class to class. Certain facets of teaching take time—sometimes several semesters—to develop to one's satisfaction. Managing classroom behavior is definitely one of those aspects. On-the-job training is the only way to come to grips with how you want to proceed. Stay calm, be patient with yourself, and always be on the lookout for new and different ideas and strategies.

That bit of advice, in fact, applies across the board—not only for maintaining order in the classroom, but for finding your way in all phases of teaching the big class. And that process occurs not only in the lecture hall, when you are surrounded by three hundred students, but also in your office, when you are meeting with a student or with your teaching assistants or are all by yourself.

Notes

1. Elisa Carbone, *Teaching Large Classes: Tools and Strategies* (Thousand Oaks, Calif.: Sage, 1998), 4 (first quote); J. Richard Aronson, "Six Keys to Effective Instruction in Large Classes: Advice from a Practitioner," in *New Directions for Teaching and Learning: Teaching Large Classes Well*, ed. M. Weimer (San Francisco: Jossey-Bass, 1987), 32 (second quote); and Nilson, *Teaching at Its Best*, 49 (third quote). See also Davis, *Tools for Teaching*, 20–27; Heppner, *Teaching the Large College Class*, 36–37; and Lang, *On Course*, 21–42.
2. Lang, *Life on the Tenure Track*, 20–21, shares this view.
3. Ibid., 14–15.
4. Nilson, *Teaching at Its Best*, 69–72.
5. Lang, *On Course*, 23–24. See also, as Lang suggests, Emily Toth, *Ms. Mentor's Impeccable Advice for Women in Academia* (Philadelphia: University of Pennsylvania Press, 2002).
6. Davis, *Tools for Teaching*, 99.
7. Carbone, *Teaching Large Classes*, 48.
8. Lang, *On Course*, 66.
9. Nilson, *Teaching at Its Best*, 94.
10. From what I can gather from my informal (and admittedly far from comprehensive) survey of the literature, the twenty-minute attention span theory dates back to 1984, in J. G. Penner's *Why Many College Teachers Cannot Lecture* (Springfield, Ill.: Thomas, 1984).
11. For extensive discussions on disabilities in the classroom, see the Ohio State University Web site: http://ada.osu.edu/resources/fastfacts/.
12. Davis, *Tools for Teaching*, 111.
13. Ibid., 103.
14. As is surely evident by now, this is not the book to turn to for advice on using technology in the classroom. For a concise overview, see Heppner, *Teaching the Large College Class*, chap. 5.
15. Lang, *On Course*, 72–73.
16. The study is cited in Christine A. Stanley and M. Erin Porter, "Teaching Large Classes: A Brief Review of the Research," in *Engaging Large Classes: Strategies and Techniques for College Faculty*, ed. Christine A. Stanley and M. Erin Porter (Bolton, Mass.: Anker, 2002), 148.
17. John P. Roche, "The Founding Fathers: A Reform Caucus in Action," *American Political Science Review* 55 (December 1961): 799–816. The article, under the title "The Convention as a Case Study in Democratic Politics," was reprinted in Leonard W. Levy, ed., *Essays on the Making of the Constitution* (New York: Oxford University Press, 1969), 175–212; see the "Editor's Note," 175–78, for Levy's critical remarks.
18. Carbone, *Teaching Large Classes*, chap. 9, is especially good on managing student behavior.

CHAPTER 3

Outside the Lecture Hall

On a Thursday evening midway through the semester, twenty-five of my three hundred students in HIST 106 sat packed together in a seminar room waiting for discussion section to start. Standing in the middle of the circle was their TA, Sam, chatting casually with a few students. At 5:00 sharp, Sam asked the students to pass forward their reading guide answers. An energy then filled the room almost immediately. It started with Sam taking out a small rubber ball and bouncing it furiously, either in front of him or off the wall to the side. I thought immediately of Captain Queeg's compulsive habit of rubbing together two metal balls with that awful clicking sound. The students loved it, however. "Why did Vaught assign this book?" asked Sam. Hands shot up in the air, as apparently every discussion began with this question. "To torture us," said the first respondent to a round of laughter. "To have us read a satire of American culture and the vacuity of American middle-class life in the 1920s," said another, matching almost word-for-word my description of *Babbitt* from the first day of class (bless her heart). And off they went, with the ball and a flurry of ideas bouncing around for a full fifty minutes of stimulating discussion.

Not all discussion sections go as smoothly as this, of course. Indeed, Sam is an especially gifted discussion leader and, having worked with me for several semesters, felt completely at ease with my scheme of things. His example, however, serves as a vivid reminder of the importance of discussion sections. They can turn a one-dimensional course (instructor–students) into one with four dimensions (instructor–students, teaching assistant–students, instructor–teaching assistants, and teaching assistants themselves). This format, moreover, allows me to assign more challenging readings, exams, and papers, and, most important, allows students to discuss them at length in an active, cooperative, and collaborative environment.

Throughout the semester, I observe these discussion sections, evaluate the discussion leaders' progress, help them craft essay questions for exams, and, in general, mentor them by example as well as with hands-on training. Much of what is involved in teaching the big class, in other words, takes place outside the lecture hall—not only supervising teaching assistants, but also composing take-home paper topics, constructing multiple-choice exams, and meeting with students during office hours.

Working with TAs

For what kind of boss would you prefer to work? Someone who dictates your every move, pays excessive attention to every last detail, and avoids delegating any meaningful decisions? Or someone who lays out the broad parameters of the task at hand, steps aside, and then trusts your judgment and ability to get the job done? Surely it is the latter—especially for academics, who value the personal freedoms that come with teaching and research. Yet academics can be micromanagers of the worst kind when it comes to working with their teaching assistants. The very freedoms that they enjoy often prevent them from relinquishing control of their classes to graduate students. At some level, all professors think that their classes—no matter how large—would be better if they taught every discussion section, graded every paper, and saw every troubled student in office hours. Throw in the fact that this peculiar manager-employee relationship includes built-in age and power differences, and you have the makings of a classic workplace paradox: While employees easily recognize and resent micromanagement, micromanagers rarely view themselves as such and instead regard their management style merely as highly organized and tightly structured.

Taken to its logical extreme, this can have the effect of every faculty member thinking that every other faculty member (except him- or herself, of course) is a micromanager—the end result being that the graduate students/teaching assistants fail to develop their skills very much or to grow and learn as teachers. I know all this intimately from my own personal experience and observations. I began my career in the classroom as a micromanager extraordinaire and have only gradually learned to loosen the reins. I may not always succeed, but I no longer try to control my teaching assistants. Instead, I seek to empower them to experiment, take responsibility, share authority, and otherwise engage themselves in their teaching.

Those teaching assistants who have taken my seminars tend not to be surprised by my management strategy. I take a decisively hands-off approach in graduate teaching. During each meeting, a graduate student presents the book of the week, followed by a free-flowing discussion for at least a half hour. No matter how chaotic things get, I stay out of it and let them sort things out for themselves. That way, even when I do step in later (usually in the role of devil's advocate), the graduate students feel that they have uncovered the main themes and concepts, rather than having them spoon-fed from above. I strongly believe that graduate students need to be encouraged to think independently and to feel independent from the outset. There are risks involved with such an approach. In a seminar, students can get frustrated—especially those who have been trained to think that the objective is to figure out what the professors want and then shovel it back to them. As teaching assistants, some would prefer to just do as they are told. And if you give them a long enough leash, they will occasionally trip over it and require help getting back on their feet. Nonetheless, the rewards are well worth the risks—for them and for me.

Trust is the key issue, and trust between professors and teaching assistants cannot be established overnight. The first step is to have an introductory meeting a few days before the term starts. By then I have already e-mailed them a draft of the syllabus, asking them to read it carefully and be ready to ask questions and provide feedback. This turns an otherwise routine, even mundane, review of the course content, policies, procedures, and activities into a substantive discussion of how to proceed. Rarely does a semester go by without the teaching assistants themselves offering valuable suggestions that prompt me to revise the syllabus—from points of clarification to entirely new policies. Until a few semesters ago, for example, I had not included an actual grade for discussion (which now counts for 10 percent), but the TAs insisted that it would help them motivate students to participate. I am still not sure if the change itself has made much of a difference, but it sent the TAs an important message: From day one, their opinions matter and are integral to the success of the course.

The most pressing topic for this first meeting is the writing workshop that TAs conduct in their discussion sections during the first week of class (it also incorporates reading and taking notes). In this meeting, discussions on how to proceed are especially fruitful if one or two of the TAs have worked for me before, as they tend to have plenty of ideas they want to show off. I help them out on the first day of class by giving the students two assignments for the writing workshop: Study the syllabus, especially the "guidelines for writing papers," and come prepared to discuss it; and write down (to be handed in) three tips for your peers from your own experience on note taking, reading, and writing. That gets the discussions started, but the burden of their success still falls on the TAs. Here are some of the better suggestions for writing papers that have come out of these initial discussions with TAs over the years:

Visualize What should a three-page paper look like? In addition to an introduction and conclusion, there is room left for about five or six paragraphs—which is to say that the essay should be constructed around five or six distinct ideas. Too many paragraphs of two or three sentences each indicate a mere listing of ideas with little development of them; and too few paragraphs approaching (or exceeding) a page in length are generally a sign that several ideas are running together.

Thesis The paper should make an explicit *argument*—which means that somewhere in the introduction should be a statement that begins, "I am arguing that . . ." But wait! My fourth commandment in the writing guidelines says not to use the first person. So, after composing the key statement, students should simply go back and delete the "I am arguing that" part. After all, which sounds more assertive: "I am arguing that the sky is blue" or "The sky is blue"? I rest my case.

Do Not Shortchange Yourself Students should read the book carefully, of course. But that will not matter if they do not make it clear to the grader that they have read the book carefully. How should they do this? In support of their arguments, they should write about *specific* and *concrete* events and issues in the book.

They should, moreover, not assume that their grader has read the book.

Quotations Students often assume the more quotations the better, but this is a fallacy in most cases. In fact, the entire paper can be written without any quotations and still get an A. Quotations by themselves explain little. Writers should not leave it up to their readers to figure out the meaning or significance of the quotation. Quotations are more ornamental than explanatory. They work best when used to top off an already clear explanation rather than as explanatory devices themselves.

Language Students should use their own voices when writing. Not too informal—e.g., "Like, you know, that *Out of This Furnace* book was awesome, man." But please, not too academic either—e.g., "The meaning of the discourse, when properly deconstructed, is highly significant."

More Thesis "Which is the better school—Texas A&M or the University of Texas?" This is sure to generate spirited discussion. On the whiteboard, write down, in ledger style, the pros and cons of each. A&M will get the most positive reaction, of course, but students invariably bring up the better nightlife, football team, etc., at their rival UT. Then have the students construct a collective thesis statement to answer the question. At first, they will offer either/or responses—mostly "TAMU is better than UT." But gradually more subtleties will emerge: "While TAMU is superior by most measures, UT has certain strengths as well."

Do these sorts of activities actually help students with their writing? A little bit, perhaps. The fact is that the TAs can talk about writing in the abstract from now to the end of time and probably not get very far, no matter how imaginative they might be. The value of the first writing workshop comes from giving the TAs and students a chance to get to know one another right away while having a substantive discussion (as opposed to yet another syllabus review or a frivolous icebreaker or two). The real teaching opportunity comes midway through the semester in the *second* writing workshop, after the students have written their first paper. In the second workshop, the TAs conduct focused discussions around the four or five most glaring or recurring problems that emerged in their sections.

Three more subjects round out the first meeting with the TAs. Teaching assistants are often very close in age to their students and thus can sometimes develop, shall we say, closer-than-professional relationships. It is impossible to prevent Cupid from firing his arrows, but it is possible—and highly preferable—to insist that the amorous pair put off getting together until after the semester is over. In other words, allow no dating or anything that resembles dating. No one-on-one trips to the coffeehouse or campus seminars, and no arm-in-arm strolls across the quad. It is simply not professional and can lead to issues of harassment. By the same token, if the TAs themselves receive unwelcome forms of harassment or feel uncomfortable in any way in their discussion sections or offices, I implore them to report such things to me right away and not let them fester. Finally, I make it clear that just as I respect them, so too are they to respect their students. Far too often, faculty and graduate students derive a certain perverse pleasure from ridiculing students—the student body as a whole or even specific individuals—for not living up to their lofty standards. Now, an occasional joke does not hurt. Witness the following misplaced participle in a student paper that gave us all a good laugh: "Having killed individuals similar to his age, I feel like Caputo had a lot of guilt from the fact that the young men he was killing could easily have been him." But the point is not to make this kind of talk the norm, which serves mainly to hide our own inadequacies.

The first day of class is also an opportune time to make your teaching assistants feel welcome—and to display that directly to the students. After my initial "Howdy!" to the class, I ask them to say "Howdy!" to the TAs, whom I have instructed to sit together in the back of the lecture hall. Invariably, this second "Howdy!" does not have the same exuberance as the first, for which they get roundly scolded: "These are the folks who will be grading your exams and papers, and you just gave them a C+ 'Howdy.' Is that a good idea, do you think?" Needless to say, they respond with gusto when given a second chance. I ask the TAs to sit in the same place for the rest of the semester, and I insist that they come to every class and take notes—for their own benefit, but even more so to serve as models for the students.

After that, the teaching assistants are pretty much on their own. They know their duties and responsibilities: Conduct discussions on the books, grade the papers and exam essays, craft the essay questions on the basis of their discussions (with my assistance—as discussed below), hold regular office hours, and determine their students' final grades (again with my assistance—see Chapter 4). I am sometimes tempted to have them write up their own reading guides, but since I have already created them for most of the books I assign, I see no reason to reinvent the wheel. Along those same lines, I do not ask them to participate in making the multiple-choice portions of the exams. We do meet as a group on a weekly basis—usually Monday morning before class—to go over the week's activities and to discuss any problems or issues that have arisen the previous week. And I encourage them to see me privately whenever they feel the need.

Of most importance, I also visit one of their sections (they teach two or three sections each) twice a semester—in the fourth and eleventh weeks or thereabouts. I assure them that I am not there to bludgeon them with harsh criticism. Still, my visits inevitably change the dynamic of the classroom—for the TAs and the students, both of whom are prone to clam up in my presence. I find a corner somewhere to sit, and then quietly observe—nothing else. Even at times when I am dying to jump in, I resist, knowing that anything I say can have the effect of undermining the TA. Immediately afterward, we have a conversation that usually begins rather awkwardly (for them and for me) but ultimately proves useful. A sampling of my observations from over the years:

Sam: My rave review of him at the beginning of the chapter notwithstanding, even Sam had a weakness or two. He knew that he was good—so much so that he could get a little cocky at times. He did not really need the reading guide questions, and he sometimes skipped them altogether. But the students were then left wondering why they had put in the time and effort to do them. Sam also cared too much about having the students like him—a problem we all share, of course. As a result, he tended to grade too easily. The close relationship that TAs have with students (in contrast to the largely anonymous relationship that I have with them) often results in inflated grades. I stress to the TAs from the outset that high grades can call their credibility into question at critical moments in their careers, such as annual reviews and tenure evaluation, no matter how good they may be in the classroom. And in large classes, once the class average gets too high, it is almost impossible to bring it back down to an acceptable level by the end of the semester. In the last couple of years, consequently, I have instructed the TAs to give no first paper a grade higher than a B+, even if Ernest Hemingway appears to have written it. "Micromanagement!" I can hear you cry. Perhaps, but inflated grades have not been a problem ever since.

Emily was another sensational TA, though she could not have been any more different from Sam in style and approach. Students adored her. She cared deeply about every last one of them and came thoroughly prepared. She liked to break her sections into small groups of three or four and have each group present a short oral report (on one of the reading guide questions, for example) by the end of class. The approach, I have to say, did not impress me at first—I found it a bit condescending. But it worked exceptionally well, and the students bought into it with enthusiasm. And teaching with small groups, I later learned, is cutting-edge pedagogy.[1] "So, what do I know?" I found myself asking. In addition, Emily emerged early in the semester as a senior TA of sorts. She served as a liaison between me and the others and took it upon herself to mentor some of the others in ways that they (and I) very much appreciated. This is great when it happens on its own, but I prefer not to force it by making a formal appointment of such a position.

Peter: In contrast to Sam and Emily, Peter was not a good TA, in large part because he put so little effort into it. Or, to put it more succinctly, he blew off the semester. When I visited his discussion section, the students dibble dabbled around for a while and then left a good twenty minutes early. Steaming mad, I told him that this simply would not do—that he was cheating the students and making me look foolish in the process. He stepped things up a bit after I laid down the law, but just enough to humor me, I suspect. In retrospect, my anger stemmed in part from the fact that I had not exactly given it my all as a TA either in graduate school. Deeply into my dissertation, I often found discussion sections a waste of my time and winged them whenever possible. Peter felt the same way, no doubt. I wrote him a critical end-of-semester evaluation for the department but did not push to deny him future funding. And you know what? Peter went on to become a fine teacher in his own right upon receiving his PhD. He did, however, expose a weakness in my hands-off approach: It allows TAs to shirk their responsibilities, if they so choose.

Jerry, on the other hand, took the job very seriously and knew exactly how he wanted to proceed. Prior to my first visit, I happened to walk down the hall past one of his discussion sections and was quite taken aback by what I saw. There was Jerry, standing behind a podium, directing his section like a drill sergeant rather than a discussion leader, with his students seated around him waiting to be called on at any moment. The benefits of sitting together with one's students—in particular, minimizing authority to maximize participation—seemed so obvious to me that I had not felt the need to explain them to my TAs, until now, that is. But Jerry was adamant that he felt more comfortable doing it his way. And sure enough, when I visited his section officially a few weeks later, he made it work. His students responded to his methods enthusiastically and discussed the books thoroughly and thoughtfully. "What do I know?" I found myself asking once again.

Sarah, unlike Jerry, was less sure of herself in the classroom and, in general, a quiet, reserved person. While she came well prepared to discussions, she was usually content to let four or five students do the talking. The thought of calling on the others directly to speak made her even more anxious than them. Sarah was no pushover, however. When an aggressive student, upset with his grade, tried to intimidate her in her office, she handled it calmly and patiently like a real pro. She reported the incident to me, as I had asked, but in the end did not need my help. Nonparticipants, however, present a more complex problem with no simple answer. Do you call on them like Jerry or follow Sarah's take-them-as-they-are approach? The former runs the risk of humiliating truly shy people, while the latter often draws the ire of the talkers, who feel that the others benefit from their contributions without contributing themselves. How does one even distinguish between slackers and the truly meek?[2]

My own undergraduate experience was much closer to Sarah's. In an American literature seminar, for example, I spoke only once the entire semester. In a discussion of Henry James's *The Portrait of a Lady*, my response to the affluent characters' deep and troubled lives was something to the effect of, "If they all just went out and got jobs they'd be much better off." I can still see everyone in the room staring at me in bewilderment as I retreated back into my cocoon. In my first seminar in graduate school, I was so self-conscious about not talking that I went to see the professor. "Don't worry about it," he said. "You'll talk when you're ready." That sage advice has guided me ever since. You simply cannot force people to speak. Yet others, including Jerry, do just the opposite with equal or greater success.[3] It just goes to show you, once again, that there is no one right way to teach. To me, this translates into letting TAs, as much as possible, find their own way, as opposed to my way.

Bob offers one more useful example. Neither a stander (like Jerry) nor a sitter (like most of the others), Bob was a stroller—on the move all over the room from start to finish. This again was not my preferred style, but Bob proved very effective, especially when he would walk right up to the student who was talking and engage him or her face-to-face. Bob's strolling was a product of his tremendous energy, which worked for him most of the time but not always. He could not, for example, stop himself from talking too much. Once students realize that you will eventually answer your own questions for them if they just wait long enough, they will fall into wait mode instinctively.

Bob's hyper energy also manifested itself in his essay questions for the exams, which generally were too long and unfocused—though that often characterizes many TAs' first efforts. The art of crafting essay questions rarely comes naturally. I want the TAs to ask questions that directly reflect the discussions they had in their sections, not generic questions about the readings. A few days before the exam (which are scheduled on discussion days), I have the TAs send me drafts of their essay questions, and it usually takes two or three e-mail exchanges to nail down the final version. The following is a typical exchange:

> Dr. Vaught,
> Here is my first shot at the Beals question:
>> Melba Pattillo Beals writes about how African Americans were inspired by Mahatma Gandhi and his nonviolent form of resistance to achieve their aims of equality and civil rights. Using examples from Beals's story, describe whether nonviolence is easier or less easy than violent confrontation and struggle—especially for a "warrior." Can nonviolence work in all societies and cultures? If so, why, and if not, why not? Describe what was going on in the United States in the 1950s that gave

> African Americans hope that their nonviolent approach could
> succeed.
> Thanks, Bob

This is a real doozy, I remember thinking—long-winded, not altogether clear, and rather awkwardly phrased. Telling him all those
things at once, however, would more likely discourage than help
him. So, I start with some encouragement and just one piece of
advice.

> Hi Bob,
> I really like the Beals question. It's challenging—but then again,
> it should be challenging. I would work a bit more on the second
> sentence, however. It's a bit awkward and should be phrased in the
> past tense.
> Thanks, DV

His response:

> Dr. Vaught,
> I had some "question creep" in the editing process. Is this version
> better?
>> Melba Pattillo Beals writes about how African Americans were
>> inspired by Mahatma Gandhi and his nonviolent form of resis-
>> tance in their quest for equality and civil rights. Which would
>> have been easier for them: violent confrontation or nonvio-
>> lent resistance? Why did they choose the way they did? Using
>> examples from *Warriors Don't Cry*, describe times that Beals
>> had to choose between violence and nonviolence, and what she
>> decided to do, and why. Can nonviolence work in all societies
>> and cultures? Why or why not? Describe what was going on
>> in the United States in the 1950s that gave African Americans
>> hope that their nonviolent approach could succeed.
> Bob

Time to get more specific.

> Bob,
> Instead of "times" in the fourth sentence, say "moments" or
> "instances" or perhaps "three instances"? Plus, as I read it again,

you've got too many questions. Be more concise, even if it means getting rid of one or two things.

DV

His next try:

Dr. Vaught,

Here is version 3.0:

Melba Pattillo Beals writes about how African Americans were inspired by Mahatma Gandhi and his philosophy of nonviolence in their quest for equality and civil rights. Using incidents from *Warriors Don't Cry*, identify whether nonviolent resistance is easier or harder than violent confrontation. How can a "warrior" practice nonviolence? Can passive resistance work in all societies and cultures? Why or why not? Describe what was going on in the United States in the 1950s that gave African Americans hope that their nonviolent approach could succeed.

Bob

Time now to provide focus.

Bob,

Here's my suggestion:

Melba Pattillo Beals writes that African Americans were inspired by Mahatma Gandhi's philosophy of nonviolence in their quest for equality and civil rights. But she also entitled her book *Warriors Don't Cry*. What was it about Little Rock, Arkansas (and the South in general), that gave African Americans hope that their nonviolent approach could succeed? On the other hand, how can a "warrior" practice nonviolence? Be sure to support your arguments with specific examples from the book.

Now — you go ahead and play with it as you see fit — and then go ahead and use v. 4.0.

I've enjoyed the give and take.

DV

Other aspects of working with TAs can be far less enjoyable, starting with having to hound them occasionally to get their grading done on time. I realize that I ask a lot of my TAs, with three exams, two papers, and two or three sections of at least twenty-five students each (not to mention attending class, reading the books, and preparing for discussions). I also realize that they, of course, have work of their own to do from their seminars and dissertation research. I try to find a happy medium and ask them to get all assignments back to the students within a week. If at all possible, I advise them, grade each batch of papers or bluebooks in one sitting, even if it takes you into the wee hours of the morning. It usually takes a half hour or so to get going, and every time you stop and start again, it takes at least that long to get back into your rhythm. You are also more likely to be consistent from the first paper to the last with this approach. Hey—that's why they invented coffee, after all! There are times, however, when TAs are so loaded down with their own work that you have to make exceptions. But again, it is almost always to everyone's advantage—theirs, yours, and the students'—to return assignments as quickly as possible.

Even less enjoyable—far less—for both the TAs and me is the never-ending battle against plagiarism. College students cheat, I am sorry to say, and they cheat seemingly without a pang of conscience. The data on the subject in the national literature is straightforward and undeniable: At least three-quarters of college students in recent years admit to engaging in some form of academic dishonesty, with plagiarism often at the top of the list. Cheating is no longer merely a manifestation of individual immorality; it is deeply embedded in undergraduate culture in colleges and universities across the country.[4] Other than a mandatory clause in the syllabus (see Chapter 1) and an impassioned plea on the first day of class (see Chapter 2), what can instructors do, if anything, to stem the tide? The following incident should suffice to reveal my approach—the most controversial, perhaps, that I offer in this book.

"I've got one," said Gilbert, one of my TAs, as he walked into my office toward the end of the semester with a paper in his hand. From his dour tone, I knew immediately what he meant. This was a real whopper. Not only were there stark differences in vocabulary, composition, and style in some paragraphs as compared to others, but those that had been cut and pasted from various Internet sources still had their smaller font size and grayer background shade! I ran it through the plagiarism-detection program turnitin.com immediately, but found matches only of quoted sentences from the assigned book—which did not surprise me. Turnitin.com has fairly limited value. It searches for sequences of words, generally eight or more, and its database, however vast, does not include many online encyclopedias or journals accessible only by subscription.[5] It does not take much savvy to avoid detection. Gilbert had already googled several of the more suspicious phrases and sentences, but to no avail. We had no hard evidence, in other words, to take to the Honors Council. I asked Gilbert what grade the paper deserved even with the cribbed passages. "C/C+," he said. "Give it a D," I replied, "and see if he comes in." He never did. That was enough for me; case closed.

There was a time when I would have pursued suspected plagiarists more diligently. Several years ago, for example, my TA discovered five papers on *Babbitt* that had all been lifted from the same free "custom essay" site on the Internet. Rather than confront the perpetrators directly, I announced in front of the entire class that if the dirty five turned themselves in over the next twenty-four hours, we would reduce their punishment from failing the class to failing just the paper. Thirteen guilty consciences confessed! While my TA and I basked in our glory for a while, eventually I began considering whether I should even assign books like *Babbitt*, which are all over the Internet (just try googling "Babbitt papers"). But then I decided I'll be damned if I'm going to let cheaters dictate my choice of course readings.

Since then, in fact, I have lost much of my patience with plagiarists and as a result have devoted minimal energy to hunting them down. It is just not worth it. If students think that cheating is OK after everything the TAs and I tell them, then so be it. We are not police investigators, and we all have better things to do with our time. Defeatism? Perhaps. But I prefer to see it as a realistic response to the culture of cheating that plagues us.

It seems as though more students complain every semester as well, though I can offer no hard data to support that claim. But it stands to reason that the larger the class, the more complaints, the vast majority of which concern grades. Do the math: If you get two or three complaints in a class of twenty-five, how many will you get in a class of three hundred? Fortunately (for instructors), the TAs, bless their souls, provide the first line of defense. Fewer than 10 percent of student complaints reach me, I would guess. I advise the TAs to field them just as Sarah did with the aggressive student who tried to intimidate her—calmly, patiently, and professionally. It simply does not pay to get visibly angry with a student, no matter how angry they may actually make you. I also give the TAs the authority to change grades on the spot if students can make convincing arguments. If the two parties reach an impasse, then the TA sends the student to me, but rarely will they get satisfaction. Even if the student appears to have a case, I am still likely to back up the TA. I remember what it was like as a TA to have the professor side with the student (often just to get them out of the office, I suspected). Not only am I loyal to the TAs, but I also realize that a single paper or essay question cannot be assessed effectively in isolation of the others. The TAs have the perspective to make the proper judgment, not me.

This brings us to the important issue of grade subjectivity, which becomes especially controversial in large classes with several teaching assistants. "My TA is harder than yours" is the refrain one constantly hears. "Your grade in Vaught's 105 depends upon your TA; it's completely unfair," insisted one particularly frustrated student in his course evaluation. It *is* unfair, especially if fair means consistency across the board. But consistency across the board is not possible even if one person is doing all the grading, let alone six—let alone the twenty or so instructors and dozens of TAs who teach U.S. history survey in my department every semester. Grading philosophies and practices are all over the map, and no doubt they vary even more widely from one history department to another. Grades only *seem* more subjective when six TAs are working in the same course, but they are subjective *period*. No matter how much students might complain, therefore, you cannot worry about how other people grade. As one wise teacher put it, "Grades are like teaching styles. We are never going to be all the same, and that's just fine. Students will benefit from exposure to different styles and different philosophies. It forces them to think about their education a little bit."[6] Such an explanation will rarely satisfy a disgruntled student, of course. All we can do is try to be reasonable and fair, give them the grades we think they deserve, and stand by them (and each other).

I am proud to stand by my TAs (well, most of the time and in most cases). Teaching the big class requires teamwork. In any given semester, the success of the course depends on the quality of the team—on how well we communicate, plan, carry out our responsibilities, and achieve our objectives. When it all comes together, team teaching with TAs can be very fulfilling. Admittedly, I sometimes look with envy at my colleagues in the department who rarely or never "manage" graduate student teachers, but in truth, I would not have it any other way.

In the Office

Not all tasks outside the lecture hall fall to the TAs. In my survey courses, I handle the objective part of the tests, the topics for the outside papers, and more than a few students during my office hours, with no one to rely on but myself.

Tests While multiple-choice tests are easy to grade, they take a long time to prepare—much more time than essay exams. Though often criticized for measuring only recall of basic facts or rote memorization, multiple-choice tests can, in fact, assess whether students have mastered complex concepts, ideas, and themes. They are not easy to write, however. The sheer complexity of the English language can make questions that seem utterly straightforward to you utterly ambiguous to students. Most new instructors (myself included fourteen years ago) make them way too hard or way too easy at first—both of which can get you in hot water. Give very few As and Bs but lots of Ds and Fs and you will become the devil incarnate, while 50 percent As will blow your class average to smithereens. To find the right balance, it took me four or five semesters and several lessons learned, including these:

Do not wait until the night before to make the exam. Instead, spread out the work. Take twenty minutes after every lecture to draft three or four questions while the classroom experience—what you emphasized, what you left out, what questions students asked—is still fresh in your mind.

The alternative answers must be unmistakably wrong but not too obvious. Do not give students any freebies. Make sure three of the answers are incorrect, but make them appealing and plausible as well by incorporating recognizable language from the lectures. Compare the following questions:

7. A new system of labor relations in the 1920s in which large companies began providing unemployment benefits, pension plans, and insurance to employees was known as
   a) the Fourteen Points.
   b) the Red Scare.
   c) welfare capitalism.
   d) the National Recovery Administration.

7. A new system of labor relations in the 1920s in which large companies began providing unemployment benefits, pension plans, and insurance to employees was known as
   a) collective bargaining.
   b) the installment plan.
   c) welfare capitalism.
   d) associationalism.

The first set of answers will fool very few students, even those who did not study. Only *c* comes from the pertinent lecture, making it easily identifiable by simple process of elimination. All four concepts in the second set, by contrast, were discussed during the same half hour on the same day. As a result, nearly 20 percent of the class missed this one the last time I gave it—most of them choosing *a* or *d*.

Try not to give away the best choice by making it longer, more detailed, or filled with more qualifiers than the alternatives. Over 90 percent got this one right because *c* seemed such an obvious choice (although five to ten guessers chose *d*):

22. Bacon's rebellion is best understood as
    a) Indians rebelling against indentured servants.
    b) backcountry planters slaughtering Indians to enhance the fur trade.
    c) an army of disgruntled small planters, indentured servants, and slaves attempting to turn the planter elite–dominated world upside down.
    d) a famous pig revolt in New England.

It never hurts to throw in a few true-false questions covering concepts and themes, such as these:

14. The Great Awakening promoted the ideal of equality throughout the American colonies while the Enlightenment reinforced
deferential thinking.

6. Postwar prosperity in the United States and the Cold War were
two mutually exclusive developments.

While students often object to negative wording, it is much
easier to construct three right answers than three plausible wrong
answers. Just be sure to underline or italicize the key word (usually
except or *not*) so as to minimize confusion. For example:

9. Which of the following did *not* characterize the Scopes trial?
    a) The slick tactics of defense attorney Clarence Darrow per-
       suaded the jury to find Scopes innocent.
    b) It revealed the deep cultural conflicts between modernist
       and fundamentalist Protestants.
    c) It centered on the conflict between science and religion.
    d) Almost immediately, it was considered "the trial of the cen-
       tury."

Use "all the above" or "none of the above" to your advantage
(students who are guessing will often choose it):

23. Liberalism in the 1960s
    a) was associated most closely with Barry Goldwater.
    b) was a political orientation that continued FDR's New Deal,
       but more cautiously.
    c) believed in the use of federal power to ensure the public
       welfare at home and to protect American interests abroad.
    d) none of the above

Be sure to include three or four especially difficult questions,
such as this:

12. Who among the following would be least likely to have dinner
    with the other three?
    a) Joseph McCarthy
    b) Alger Hiss

    c) Richard Nixon
    d) John F. Kennedy

(Stumped? McCarthy, Nixon, and Kennedy, in contrast to Hiss, were staunch anti-Communists.)

    Be sure to vary the position of the best answer. Smart students know to choose *b* or *c* when in doubt because test makers choose that position most often. With thirty questions, make sure there are seven or eight answers for all four possibilities.

    Finally, good questions will achieve the right balance, even when humor is the intended objective:

13. The Bay of Pigs invasion
    a) showcased the CIA's military expertise.
    b) intensified the growing mistrust between Kennedy and Khrushchev.
    c) strengthened Kennedy's reputation in international affairs.
    d) was an effort to overthrow the new Soviet-supported regime in East Berlin.

Nearly 10 percent—most of whom probably (hopefully?) missed class—chose *a*.

    Indeed, coming to class is the key. If students are able to schlep their way through a multiple-choice exam without really studying and still come out OK, then the exam—and, by extension, the class—loses much of its legitimacy. This is precisely why I assign no mandatory textbook, post no lecture notes online, offer no extra credit, conduct no review sessions, and take no (or very little) attendance. Sometimes it takes them until after the first exam, but students eventually learn that they cannot do well, or even keep their heads above water, without coming to class—every class. It is their responsibility to understand the course content and mine to make it worth their while. One student expressed her gratitude for this implicit agreement—"Vaught's doctrine," it might modestly be called—in her course evaluation: "Dr. Vaught is actually a really good prof. He's passionate about his topic, and generally managed to hold my interest. He doesn't get fixated on one point and drone on about it the whole class. He writes the lecture outline on the board before class and sticks to it very well. Overall, I'd recommend this class because it was a good freshman reality-check class. It forced me to do homework and go to class." I could not ask for more, frankly.

Paper Topics As with multiple-choice questions, composing effective paper topics is also an acquired skill and just as critical for carrying out Vaught's doctrine of shared responsibilities. The best students will be able to write strong papers no matter how the prompts are written, but most need clear, focused, and specific instructions. Consider the following three examples:

> In the first half of *Out of This Furnace* (pp. 3–217), Thomas Bell narrates the story of two generations of an immigrant Slovak family living in the steel-mill town of Braddock, Pennsylvania, during the late nineteenth and early twentieth centuries. In your well-developed, well-organized three-page essay, compare the expectations and experiences of first- and second-generation immigrants, as portrayed by George Kracha and his son-in-law Mike Dobrejcak. In your response, address at least three of the following issues: work life; family, home, and community life; political consciousness; self-image; ethnic identity; perceptions of America. How do you account for the similarities and differences between generations?

> How does John Kasson account for the fact that it was Coney Island, not the great Columbian Exposition of Chicago, that best met the hunger of city people of the late nineteenth century for amusement? In your well-developed, well-organized three-page essay, be sure to support your conclusions with specific evidence — the book's photographs, in particular.

> "You're a warrior on the battlefield for your lord" (p. 57).
>   "Please, God, let me learn how to stop being a warrior. Sometimes I just need to be a girl" (p. 217).
>   "I think only the warrior exists in me now. Melba went away to hide" (p. 246).
>   How would you explain to someone who had not read the book the meaning of Melba Beals's choice of the title *Warriors Don't Cry*? In your well-developed, well-organized three-page essay, consider Beals's personal, family, and religious values, the impact of integration in Little Rock, and her experiences during her junior year at Central High.

The topics are very different in approach, which is a good idea. Each one should make students think about the books and address the topics in new and challenging ways. Because *Out of This Furnace* is a novel and thus it is more difficult to understand its historical significance, the prompt explicitly lays out the generational theme and even provides a clear sense of how to proceed. A good thesis statement for this question should practically write itself. The Kasson question, in contrast, is wide open, stating only what should be obvious: Employ the book's numerous photographs as evidence for one's arguments. Students are left to their own devices to find central and supporting themes for their papers. The Beals topic is the most literary of the three, with the focus on the three quotations. I first assigned it without the "consider" instruction at the end but found that students needed the extra guidance. It is a good idea, in fact, to keep notes on the successes and pitfalls of each paper topic to consult in subsequent semesters if revision is necessary. As with multiple-choice questions, revision will most likely be necessary when you are first starting out and even later when you develop new topics.

Yet all three topics share similar features as well. First and foremost, they all ask for *theme papers* — for students to take an explicit position. The instructions with regard to composition—"well-developed, well-organized," "support your conclusions with specific evidence," etc.—hearken back to the "Guidelines for Writing Papers" at the end of the syllabus. It is my hope, in fact, that the prompts will remind students (if the TAs have not already done so) to review that important document before they start writing. The topics are also designed to complement the reading guides. Indeed, if students have a good grasp of those sets of questions, particularly after discussing them in section, then they should be well-equipped to tackle the papers.[7]

Office Hours One would like to think that more time spent crafting good exam and paper questions would mean less time spent with students in office hours later, but alas, such is probably not the case. Even though my small army of TAs on the front lines shields me from the constant barrage of student complaints, I, too, receive my share of visits. Students sometimes prefer to come down to the lectern right after class to ask questions, when I am usually dog-tired. Unless the question is straightforward and easy to answer, I ask the student to meet me during office hours or to make an appointment. I do not want to risk giving a misleading response that I might regret later. Under just such conditions, I recently told a student, for example, that he could hand in a paper a week late, only minutes after his TA had told him just the opposite. I reversed my decision later that afternoon, but that left both the student and the TA upset with me, and rightly so from the TA's perspective. Haste (amid exhaustion) does indeed make waste.

Early in the semester, several students often ask if they can record the lectures. I prefer not to have my course materials "out there" with no control over their dissemination. But the fact that they have asked (in the big auditorium, they could easily tape me without my knowing) suggests that their concerns are genuine. "Why would anyone want to hear me more than once?" I quip at first. Knowing that they are freshmen and probably anxious about the pace and intensity of the lectures, I ask them to be patient with themselves and see how things go before the first exam. Recording the lectures, I emphasize, serves mainly as a crutch for students who are unsure of themselves, and as such prevents them from learning a valuable skill—note taking—that will help them for the rest of their college careers. "If you still feel the need after the first exam, come back and talk to me about it," I conclude. No one has ever come back. Some of them (most, I hope?) walk out with the small boost of confidence that they needed, while others (just a few?) no doubt record behind my back anyway.

For many freshmen in large introductory courses, the first semester often brings a jolt of reality—on any number of issues, but especially, when they come to see me, on grades. Most newly admitted students are used to, and indeed expect, high marks, and I do not mean Bs or Cs. By rule in my recent scheme of things, none of them earn As on their first papers, and only 10 percent or so grab the brass ring on the first exam. Some conclude that their TA was simply not up to the task of recognizing their superior skills and, after speaking with them or not, bring their papers to me for a second opinion. "I've never gotten lower than a B+ before," they explain in so many words. Many then add the obligatory, "Look at all these red marks; this is not an English class." What follows is never pleasant: reading the paper right then and there while they sit and stare at me. (I sometimes ask them to come back later to allow me to read it carefully, but that usually serves only to postpone the inevitable.) The papers are never As (at least, I cannot recall such an instance) and often merit, in my mind, even a lower grade than the TA gave. The impulse to cave in can be very strong, but it is in no one's best interest to do so. After praising them for their effort and initiative, I recommend that they talk again with their TA to make sure they know why they received the sub-par grade and, even more important, that they know how to improve on their second paper. I also remind them that they can bring a draft to their TA in advance for their comments. Not everyone—far from it, in fact—earns As in college history courses. Eventually, they come to grips with that and get used to Bs and Cs, but usually not until after their introductory courses.

Even more challenging can be office visits from athletes—especially football and basketball players, who often have (or think they have) the most at stake. I could go on at some length, but instead I offer one example to make my point. A few years ago, I had Jimmy, a starting wide receiver on the football team, in my HIST 106 class in the spring semester. Jimmy rarely came to class, did miserably on all the assignments, and failed the class—and by quite a bit. I had assumed that he did not need the course to maintain his eligibility, and so had he, apparently. But early in June, he came into my office in a panic, telling me that failing 106 would prevent him from playing in the fall. "Pleeeeeeeeeaze, Dr. Vaught," he begged, literally on his knees. "All my other teachers have changed their grades." That rather dubious claim failed to convince me, and after considerable pleading, he finally left. Yet there was Jimmy, catching passes at Kyle Field three months later (never underestimate the ingenuity of the athletic department). Jimmy was good, but too small and not fast enough to get drafted by an NFL team. He neither reached the pros nor received much of an education, I'm afraid. Even though I held the line against him, I still feel, in some way, that I was part of the collective effort to exploit this young man's talents for the short-term interests of the university. It happens all the time, but when you teach the big class, you often get a front-row seat to the action.

E-mail One final word of advice. Over the course of the semester, you will receive dozens upon dozens of e-mails from students on every imaginable subject, some even unimaginable. Answer them as best you can, briefly and with as little emotion as possible. We all know that e-mail, however valuable a means of communication, can sometimes give mixed messages and cause unintended harm even in the most routine, bland exchanges. With students, especially, resist the temptation to respond in kind to rude (or what appear to be rude) messages, as in the following exchange:

> Dr. Vaught,
> This is Millie Jones from History 105. Is there any way you can tell me what grade I got on the final? I know that I missed turning in one of the last major papers because I just ignorantly let it slip my mind. Did that zero combined with the final exam make me fail the course?

Already I am a bit miffed because the answers to her questions have all been covered in the syllabus and in class numerous times. But I respond briefly and without emotion, as prescribed.

> Millie,
> The short answer to your last question is yes. Quoting the syllabus: "**All graded assignments and exams must be completed to earn a passing grade.**"
> DV

She replied:

> All right I understand. However, is there any way you could let me know what my grade was on the final if it's not an inconvenience? Thank you.

I just explained that the zero on the paper makes the grade on the final exam irrelevant, but I respond anyway.

> Millie,
> I do not have the grades with me, plus the university prefers that I not discuss them with students via e-mail.
> DV

Apparently, I hit a nerve:

Dr. Vaught,
I understand that you don't have the grades on you currently and
that it's a minor inconvenience for you to get them, but I really
would like you to get me just the grade I made on the final exam.
That's all I need. Since you don't have e-learning I don't have any
idea what I made and had no way of tracking my grades throughout the semester. [I am not sure what she means by this since my
university does not allow instructors to post grades online.] Other
professors have had no problem discussing grades via e-mail. [This,
too, is not allowed.] I will be in College Station Monday. If you need
me to get the grade from you in person or pick it up somewhere
on campus, I can do that. However, since that grade was not given
to us because summer has begun, I think I have a right to at least
know what I made on the last exam.

My first impulse was to fire right back, but instead I waited a couple of hours and kept my cool.

Millie,
I will be in the office tomorrow afternoon and will send you your
grade on the final exam then.
DV

The next day:

Grade on the final exam: D

No response.

I told her the grade just to get her off my back, which I should
not have done, of course. In fact, I should have made it much more
clear from the outset that I could not discuss her grade via e-mail,
and left it at that. It just goes to show you: I am still living and
learning after all these years.

You may be thinking at this point that I find students to be
pests and seek to avoid them at all costs. Not so, I can assure you.
I find teaching large numbers of freshmen and sophomores—in
and outside the lecture hall, with and without teaching assistants—to be challenging, stimulating, and satisfying. Instructors
of large classes, if you will please excuse my preaching, should be
immensely grateful for the opportunity to inspire so many young

people at once. But to restate the obvious, large is fundamentally different from small. Every semester, unforeseen problems, complaints, incidents, and situations will emerge—count on it—that you, as captain of the ship, will be called upon to resolve. And every semester, familiar problems, complaints, incidents, and situations will reemerge that you—again—will be called upon to resolve. And every semester, you will make some painful mistakes along the way. Such is one's fate when teaching the big class. It is sure to be a wild ride. Enjoy it.

Notes

1. Lang, *On Course*, 104–26; and Davis, *Tools for Teaching*, 147–65.
2. There can be any number of reasons why students choose not to participate; see Rebekah Nathan, *My Freshman Year: What a Professor Learned by Becoming a Student* (New York: Penguin, 2005), 92–95.
3. For a compelling argument for calling on people, see Lang, *On Course*, 96–98.
4. Nathan, *My Freshman Year*, 123–29; and Lang, *On Course*, 198–99.
5. John Royce, "Trust or Trussed? Has Turnitin.com Got It All Wrapped Up?" *Teacher Librarian Magazine* 30 (April 2003): 26–30.
6. Quoted in Lang, *Life on the Tenure Track*, 81. On grading more generally, see Lang's insightful chapter on grading in that book, 68–82.
7. See Davis, *Tools for Teaching*, 213–21, for more on designing effective writing assignments.

CHAPTER 4

Finishing Up

By the last week of the semester, I am almost always filled with mixed emotions, from "No way—you must be kidding" to "Thank god it's almost over." It is both a hectic and an exhausting time for everyone—students, TAs, and professors alike. The winter or summer break is looming, but no one can afford to think about such pleasantries just yet—we're all too busy. Faculty are rushing to get through the last topics of their courses, TAs have tons of grading to do, and students are beginning to think about finals. If at all possible, give your students and TAs a break with two or three weeks to go. I have taken up the practice of canceling discussion sections in the second-to-last week of class. The surprise announcement a few days earlier invariably brings thunderous applause and a welcome sense of relief—not to mention a long weekend away from HIST 106. For instructors, the temptation is to just let their courses peter out with no proper ending or sense of closure. But I urge you not to cop out and instead end the semester with a bang. Go out swinging. Ham it up. Impart great wisdom. There will still be mundane matters to attend to—most notably final grades and evaluations—but do your best to make the last week memorable.

The Last Lecture

Just as the first day of the semester should, in some way, stir students' intellectual curiosity about the subject matter of the course, so too should the final day encourage their continued interest in the subject. Let neither be routine or perfunctory. Gear up and make the last lecture special so that students will walk away excited about history.[1] This does not mean pile it on. The last thing students need at this stage of the game is more stuff for the final exam. They are, to say the very least, not receptive to new information at this point, and in fact, many of them are running on empty or running scared. As I mentioned in Chapter 1, my last lecture for HIST 106 is on Watergate. I recount the long, convoluted sequence of events from the break-in to Nixon's resignation, which is dramatic, indeed sensational, all by itself. But my primary aim is less to provide knowledge than to be provocative and, dare I say, inspirational. Only one or two questions from the lecture will appear on the final exam, and they are very easy to answer for anyone who attended. The theme, as stated in the lecture subtitle, is "the politics of cynicism," and for the only time all semester, the approach is autobiographical. After all, this was my time—when I came of age politically. To illustrate, here are two excerpts, one from the beginning and one from the end (see Appendix C for the lecture outline):

> American politics is a dirty game—always has been and always will be. Why? The answer is pretty easy, actually. In American politics, there are only two parties and you get nothing for coming in second. Nothing. Zippo. Nada. You can have all the most virtuous motives and objectives in the world for wanting to become president, but if you don't get elected, they don't matter. Winner-take-all is a system that pushes candidates to do just about anything. Previous presidents from Andrew Jackson to Abraham Lincoln to Woodrow Wilson to FDR on up to Kennedy and LBJ all have abused their powers in search of ways to discredit their opponents. We constantly hear complaints about negative campaigning today. But folks, that's been the story of American politics since almost day one. If your opponent calls you a schmuck and you don't call him a schmuck right back, the odds are overwhelming that you will come in second—which is to say, nowhere.
>
> Now, in that context, it's fashionable to say that the only thing that Richard Nixon did wrong was that he got caught. And there's some truth to that. But there's also a whole heck of a lot more to it than that. Others have abused their power in the quest for political gain—but Nixon did it more—took it to new heights, or lows, depending on how you look at it. He did it more zealously, he did it more recklessly, and he did it seemingly without conscience. It's now very commonplace, but Nixon was really the first president to start running for reelection the day he first stepped into the White

House. By all accounts, he was obsessed with his own political status. He had lost the presidential election in 1960 as well as the California gubernatorial election in 1962, and had won the presidency in 1968 but only by the slimmest of margins. Looking toward 1972, he would leave no stone unturned.

Watergate, the great constitutional crisis of the early 1970s, was a direct result of Nixon's ruthless political tactics. Nonetheless, we should not see Watergate as consisting of only the evil deeds of one person and one unlawful act. Watergate was not an isolated incident. It was part of a broad pattern of illegality and misuse of power that flourished in the crisis atmosphere of the Vietnam War and broader Cold War. America's obsession with communism — the containment of communism in particular — cannot be overstated. Presidents from Truman to Nixon lied, cheated, and obfuscated and all felt fully justified to do so under the guise of the Soviet threat — just as Johnson did in the Gulf of Tonkin incident, as we saw the other day. Even when such indiscretions were exposed, the American people often justified them for the same reasons. The end always seemed to justify the means. . . .

But Congress could not legislate away Watergate's most significant legacy — the wave of cynicism that swept the country. The public was already distrustful of government in the wake of Vietnam, and the Watergate saga seemed to confirm the suspicions of many Americans that politicians were hopelessly corrupt and that the federal government was out of control. Two bumper stickers that were popular during the 1976 presidential campaign spoke volumes: "Don't vote. It only encourages them," said one. "The lesser of two evils is still evil," said the other.

That cynicism about politics, I think most of us will agree, still persists today. Ronald Reagan gave many Americans hope, but that seems to have been short-lived; and the Gulf War of the early '90s and the immediate aftermath of 9/11 renewed a sense of patriotism, but that too seems to have been short-lived. Barack Obama built his entire campaign around the politics of cynicism, his rhetoric centering around the line, "We're not blue states; we're not red states; we are the United States." But so far, anyway, it would be difficult to argue that he has managed to bring the country together.

All you have to do, it seems to me, is to look at how many of us actually bother even going to the polls today — it's still just over 50 percent in national elections, even with all the hoopla of the last campaign, and considerably less than that in state, local, and off-year elections. And, if I may editorialize, why the hell should we? Each election we hear the same old, tired rhetoric from both sides: "I'm for education; I'm for the family; I'm for the economy." Give me a break. In many ways, it's like a replay of the late nineteenth century with politics centering around personalities and petty scandals, rather than on issues that might wake us all up in some profound way. "Who cares" seems to be the overriding sentiment of the day when it comes to politics, and in many ways it's a difficult sentiment to argue with. Now again, some would argue that the current twin crises of war and recession, along with the activist bent of the current administration, will push politics to the forefront of people's minds and transform the politics of cynicism. We'll see.

On the other hand, throughout History 106, we've seen what politicians are capable of doing if they don't believe they're being monitored — monitored by us. And the only way to hold them accountable is to vote them out of office as we see fit. I for one have been voting since 1976, and I have yet to vote for a candidate in a presidential election whom I have been truly, emotionally excited about — in the way my parents were truly, emotionally excited about JFK and that my grandparents were truly, emotionally excited about FDR. In my mind, I have always voted for, as the bumper sticker put it, "the lesser of two evils" and I often think that is my destiny as an American citizen.

So there's a dilemma in our particular political age that we all have to confront: Do you just say, "The hell with it," which again, is a perfectly rational response, I think, or do you try to become involved, in some way, to make yourself feel like a contributing member of American politics? I hope that if nothing else, your 106 experience has provided you historical perspective to help you with that decision.

On behalf of your teaching assistants — [point to and name them] — we have very much enjoyed having you this semester, and wish you the very best on the final and in your future endeavors here at Texas A&M University and beyond.

A round of applause usually follows (not always but most of the time, and sometimes louder than others) before everyone departs and goes about their respective business. I may never fully achieve my lofty objectives for the last lecture, but I sure have fun trying.

Evaluations

While the last lecture seeks to end the course with an exclamation point, it is something of a misnomer. "Last" does not mean all done. 'Tis the season for evaluation, after all. Students evaluate their instructors; teaching assistants their students; and instructors their teaching assistants. For all parties concerned, it can be a time of apprehension, anxiety, and even resentment. We would all do well to make it a time of self-evaluation as well.

At my university, student evaluations may be administered at any time in the last three or four weeks of the semester—as soon as the rating forms appear in one's mailbox. I prefer to wait until the second-to-last day of the term (the last day is already reserved for the last lecture, of course), if for no other reason than because they are *course* evaluations, not three-quarters-of-a-course evaluations. The instructions do not designate a specific portion of the class period to distribute the forms, but if you wait until the last fifteen minutes (which is tempting if you are trying to get through material), students will treat them as optional and leave right away or shortly thereafter. Hand them out at the beginning of class, instead. It is wise to take a couple of minutes to explain to students the purpose of these ratings: Administrators use them to evaluate instructors and, even more important, instructors use them to evaluate themselves. "Please take them seriously because I take them seriously," I emphasize. Because our forms have no place for written comments, I ask students to flip them over and answer two additional questions on the back: "What did you like about the course?" and "What would you do to make it better?" And if the course had teaching assistants, they answer the same two questions with regard to their discussion sections. Some professors cancel the rest of the class, toss candy to the audience, throw heaps of praise on their students—anything to squeeze out a higher rating. My advice would be to simply leave the room, allow students to finish, and let the chips fall where they may.

Not that I do not understand the temptation to grovel. I recall vividly looking through the packet of student evaluations from my first HIST 105 class at Texas A&M a few weeks after the semester had ended. Right on top was a computerized summary of my performance. Using a scale of 1 to 5 (strongly disagree, disagree, undecided, agree, strongly agree), the students had responded to fifteen standardized statements ranging from "The instructor seemed well prepared for each class" to "The instructor stimulated my interest in the subject" to "The amount of work and/or reading was reasonable." The summary form provided my "mean score" for each item and, though it took me a while to find it way up in the right-hand corner, my "overall mean" as well. It felt demeaning, I must say, to have an assessment of my work for the entire semester reduced to filling in bubbles, though it soon dawned on me that is exactly how we evaluate our students in large introductory courses for a good portion of their final grade.

Even more demeaning was the fact that my 4.12 (pretty good, I thought at first glance) proved to be considerably lower than my department's overall mean of 4.32. Two full tenths of a point lower—"This cannot be good," I remember thinking with considerable trepidation. I went back to the summary form and closely examined my scores, trying to figure out where I had gone wrong and how I could make up ground the next semester. I got a 3.88 on the amount of work I assigned. "Lazy students," I concluded immediately. "What? A 3.85 for 'stimulating my interest in the subject.' But I stimulated the hell out of them," I thought to myself. "Ungrateful students." Angry at them and fearful of what my colleagues would think of my score, I resented the fact that I had been subjected to such an obviously unreliable method of evaluation (3.85 for stimulation, indeed). But I have learned over the years that if you use these scores to measure your progress as a teacher, you will drive yourself crazy. A score of 4.32 really is exactly two-tenths of a point higher than 4.12, but does it really indicate a tangible difference in the quality of teaching? Of course not. A score of 4.5 is significantly better than one of 3.5, I suppose, but a range much narrower than that does not tell you very much. If you go up or down five- or six-tenths of a point from one semester to the next, in other words, do not worry about it (or be overly pleased).

Do student evaluation forms have any value, then? A couple of years ago, I served on a committee for the College of Liberal Arts that considered that very question. As you might imagine, research on the subject is voluminous, equivocal, and controversial. But most studies do agree on one important point: Well-designed rating forms provide a reliable measure of student learning and teaching effectiveness *if and only if* those results are compared with other *external* measures of student learning and teaching effectiveness.

The measure of choice is to have committees of trained experts examine students' performance on course work, interview students, survey alumni, and observe instructors in the classroom— presumably for every course offered in a given semester.[2] This is all well and good for small courses at small liberal arts colleges, but it is downright impossible for large courses at large universities. As such, our committee recommended that the college do away with the rating forms altogether and instead design a series of questions for students to answer in writing, not by filling in bubbles.

We thought our solution was radical and ingenious, but deep down we knew it would not get very far with the dean's office. Why? Because at large universities like Texas A&M, promotion and tenure committees, department heads, deans, and administrators all the way up the line have little or no choice but to assess instructors' classroom performance on the basis of their teaching evaluation scores. It is neither practical nor feasible to do it any other way. In effect, large universities, knowingly or not, rely heavily on methods that have been proven to be unreliable. What does this mean for faculty, especially those on the tenure track? In most cases, depending on the institution, the rating forms have limited professional impact. One's tenure, promotion, or retention rarely hinges on one's student evaluation scores. Still, the cynic in me wants to tell tenure-track faculty a surefire method to go after stellar evaluations: Have three exams; give your students sky-high grades on the second one; and then, after they have done the evaluations, slam them on the third one to get your grades down. But the best advice, I think, is to try to stay within a range that does not call attention to your scores. In my department, anything below 4.0 is likely to bring groans from some quarters, while 4.5 or above often raises a few red flags as well.

From a practical standpoint, therefore, student evaluation forms remain an enigma. They appear exact and precise but are decisively inexact and imprecise. They are not meaningless, but their meaning is difficult, if not impossible, to ascertain. This is why I ask students to flip the forms over and answer my two questions on the back (as do many of my colleagues). I crave some sort of concrete feedback. But even then, you have to take students' responses with a grain of salt. Some will say, for example, "too much reading" no matter how many books you assign; "talks too fast" no matter how deliberately you speak; and "grades too hard" no matter how many As you give. By the same token, do not let a few hyperbolic comments such as "best class ever" or "Vaught rocks" go to your head either (though the latter are always nice). However, if a lot of students complain about a specific book, I will probably not use it again; or if a lot inform me that my voice tends to taper off at times while I lecture, I will do my best to avoid mumbling the next time.

In the end, only one person is in the best position to evaluate your performance, and that person is you. Find the time—make the time—to sit in your office alone to reflect on the semester. This is when keeping a class-by-class log becomes especially useful. Take note of which lectures, exam questions, and paper topics need significant revision. How might you manage your teaching assistants more effectively? What did they teach you? What can you do the next time to make the class better? And make sure that you actually make these revisions and implement these changes. I will never forget the time, halfway through a lecture, when I saw "This sucks" scribbled across my notes, which I had not had time to review before class. And you know what? It sucked even more the second time, especially with my own reminder staring me in the face! Listen to yourself. You know best.

The Last Meeting

The last meeting of the semester—and this time I really do mean last—is with my teaching assistants to go over the final grades of all our three hundred students. The TAs arrive fully prepared, having graded the essay portion of the final exam and determined each student's grade for the course. They read off their grades, one by one, section by section, for me to fill in yet another set of bubbles on the grade sheets. If they are at all unsure about someone's grade, we stop and discuss it as a group. Invariably the student is right between grades and too close to call. The determining factor, most often, is improvement. If the student has shown dramatic or even gradual improvement over the semester, we do not hesitate to give him or her the higher grade. In fact, we reward improvement even more than the grade scale in the syllabus indicates. For example, if someone gets a D or an F on the first exam, but As on both the second and third exams, along with good paper grades, they have earned an A, we believe, even if a straight calculation of the percentages indicates otherwise. They have shown us that the first exam was a fluke, and we treat it as such. In all, we probably discuss two to three dozen cases while I dutifully record all the grades as the TAs report them. By now, I either trust the TAs or I do not, and even in the rare cases where I am still not sure about one of them, I have little choice but to take their word at face value.

In contrast to the many who express dissatisfaction about specific paper or exam grades over the course of the semester, remarkably few students complain about their final course grades—only about five or so in most cases and never more than ten in all my semesters of teaching, even in classes of three hundred or more. I would like to chalk this up to the dividends accrued from my long-leash management style. By the end of the semester, the TAs are confident in their ability to assess their students and have become quite skilled at doing so. There is also the fact that we do not have plus and minus grades at Texas A&M, which gives the TAs more room for error. And as I have mentioned before, by now most students have become accustomed to the grades they receive. When I do receive a complaint, I listen to it carefully and reexamine the TA's records (of which I keep copies). Making the change, if necessary, involves filling out a simple form.

With the grades done and bubbles filled in, we jump in my car and head out for lunch. As with the last lecture, the temptation is to let the semester wind down with a whimper by allowing the TAs to just wander off after the last meeting. There is no better way, I can assure you, to make graduate students feel appreciated than with free food. Take them somewhere nice. Come on, splurge a little. Your reputation among the troops will skyrocket, and besides, it is just a nice thing to do. And try not to talk shop while you eat. The semester is over, after all.

All that is left are the departmental evaluations of my teaching assistants, which I try to do that afternoon, after lunch. While I adamantly guard against grade inflation in my classes, undergraduate and graduate alike, I am a pushover when it comes to my TAs. I try not to assess them against each other. After all, some of them have just finished their first semester leading discussion sections, while others were already seasoned veterans before the semester started. As long as they worked hard, took it seriously, and made progress over the course of the semester, I deem them "superior," the highest rating on our form. Since I have already sat down with them twice to discuss their performance in the classroom, I rarely feel the need to do so again at the end of the semester.

That is it. Finis. Done. The end of the semester always seems like it went by at supersonic speed and feels a little anticlimactic as well. The great thing about teaching, however, is that another adventure always awaits you the next semester, when another three hundred students and another set of TAs fill the lecture hall the first day. You may not even notice it, but with every semester that goes by, you will be that much more experienced, that much more confident, and that much more ready to knock their socks off!

Notes

1. The "last lecture" was a tradition at UC Berkeley in the early 1960s, in which instructors sought to close their courses with particularly memorable or inspirational words of wisdom. It has apparently died out over the years, however; see Heppner, *Teaching the Large College Class*, 147–50. See also Lang, *Life on the Tenure Track*, 145–46.
2. For summaries of the vast literature on student rating forms, see Lang, *On Course*, 265–82; Bain, *What the Best College Teachers Do*, 165–72; and Heppner, *Teaching the Large College Class*, 143.

(Not a) Conclusion

Usually, when a book begins with an introduction, it ends with a conclusion. Since teaching is an ongoing and uneven process of discovery, however, any definitive closing remarks would not be appropriate, it seems to me.[1] There is no end to a book like this, except that it runs out of pages. Five years from now, my experiences in the lecture hall could lead me to any number of new and different "conclusions." This book comes to a close, therefore, in the same spirit with which it began: My advice to you, colleague to colleague, comes with no strings attached. I offer it for you to take or discard at your discretion. If, along the way, I have helped jump-start a discussion on teaching the big class, I will be pleased to have met my objective. For the sake of clarity and emphasis, and to take one last crack at stimulating the conversation, I leave you with one more pep talk in five short segments.

Patience, Patience, Patience The first time you teach the big class, you *will* make mistakes—lots of them, some more serious than others, both inside and outside the lecture hall. Looking back on the first time I lectured on the coming of the Civil War, I can still feel the burn. I meant to say *sectional* conflict but out came, instead—you guessed it—*sexual* conflict. They never let me forget it. You will make mistakes with the syllabus, multiple-choice questions, supervising the TAs, final grades—everything. Come to think of it, you will also make mistakes your second time around, as well as your third, fourth, fifth . . . you get my point. The big class will test your patience for as long as you teach it. Expect that you will stumble, and learn to roll with the punches.

Everything Comes Out in the Wash This profound realization may not hit you until the very end of the semester, when you have finished the final grades. If you have structured your course so that students, in order to do well, have to come to lectures, participate in discussions, do the readings, and consult their TAs when they need help, then other decisions you spent a considerable amount of time pondering may not matter very much, if at all. It will not matter if students claimed their grandmother died, if they turned in their paper late, regularly arrived late or left early, or did not bother taking notes. The grades will all fall into place—A, B, C, D, F—with very few exceptions. The lesson? Do not sweat the little stuff because everything comes out in the wash anyway. Just make sure you remember this the next time around.

Never Let Them See You Sweat Lest you think I have some sort of fixation on sweat, I can assure you it is indeed apropos. Do you remember all those characters from that fateful day of mine fourteen years ago, when time seemed to stop during my Great Awakening lecture—the whisperers, gigglers, eaters, sleepers, note passers, clock checkers, and of course newspaper readers? I sure do. I was sweating like a pig. But you know, those characters are still out there—in fewer numbers, hopefully, but still out there nonetheless. I just do not notice them anymore. If you let yourself get rattled by such things, the big class will eat you alive. Similarly, when problems arise with students or TAs, have confidence that you will be able to resolve them. You have before; you can again. And even if they do succeed in rattling you, never let them see you sweat. It only encourages them.

Balance Teaching and research, I have come to realize, are inseparable parts of the same process. As a field of knowledge, an intellectual pursuit, and a profession, history is driven by dialogue—dialogue between historical actors, historians and primary sources, historians and students, and historians themselves. The human dimension inherent in the dialogue defines and complicates the historian's craft. History demands empirical rigor but also an acceptance and even a fondness for a process that rarely produces empirical truths. If, as I tell my students, "History is what historians say it is," then historians must be fully cognizant of past and ongoing dialogue if our contributions are to be meaningful. Whether communicating with students, colleagues, or texts, historians should not seek the final word, but instead should attempt to open up new avenues of investigation, criticism, and self-reflection. This has been a hard-earned philosophy that has developed from fourteen years of teaching, and it has served me well, both inside and outside the classroom.

But it is a philosophy. Teaching and research complement each other in the abstract, but in practice—in one's day-to-day life—teaching and research need to be separated as much as possible. The most difficult challenge for me in the early stages of my career, I found, was to budget my time properly. In that first semester, I had twenty-seven lectures to write, and that was just for one of my two classes. I could easily have made HIST 105 an around-the-clock job. But like most assistant professors, I had even more pressing research obligations. I took the advice of a senior colleague and established "teaching days" (Mondays, Wednesdays, and Fridays) and "research days" (Tuesdays and Thursdays), but I found that teaching invariably crept into every day of the week, weekends included. The trick that worked for me, ultimately, was to have a "teaching place" (my office on campus) and a "research place" (my office at home). I simply did not take teaching home or research to campus. Remember also to balance work life with private life. If that means literally scheduling time for your family, friends, recreation, and—yes—solitude, by all means do it.

Fame When you teach hundreds of students a semester, especially in a college town, you will become a local celebrity in no time at all. "Howdy, Dr. Vaught!" I hear it everywhere—not just around campus, but in restaurants, supermarkets, movie theaters, gas stations, doctors' offices—you name it. When my wife or daughter is with me, I pretend that the attention bothers me, in the same way that movie stars find their fans annoying at times. But deep down, the recognition always sends me on a giant ego trip—one that comes only from teaching the big class.

And occasionally, the amazing happens. Three years ago, I was in Norman, Oklahoma, for a conference and found myself waiting in line with several friends for a table at a crowded restaurant. I felt a tap on my shoulder and, as I turned around, there was a young, athletic-looking woman who greeted me, "Howdy, Dr. Vaught!" She then pointed across the room to a dozen other young, athletic-looking women at a large table, who roared in unison, "Howdy, Dr. Vaught!" They were all members, it turned out, of the Texas

A&M soccer team (in town for a game against the University of Oklahoma), who had taken HIST 105 with me the previous year. I turned to face my buddies, who stood before me with their mouths having dropped wide open, and said simply, "Eat your hearts out!" I ask you: Does it get any better than that?

At the risk of reducing the entire book down to one observation, it has always seemed to me that either you like being with eighteen- and nineteen-year-olds, or you do not. And when you are teaching the big class, you had better like them in droves. It is a rush like no other. Take what you learn every semester, move forward, and have a blast. Onward and upward!

Note

1. Peter Filene, *Joy of Teaching*, 132–33, among others, reached the same, well, conclusion.

Sample Syllabi

History of the United States from 1877

History 106 (sections 504–515)
Spring 2009
Texas A&M University
Dr. Vaught

Class, Instructor, and TA Information
Class Meetings: MW 12:40 to 1:30, CHEM 100 + your scheduled discussion
    section
Office: 314B HIST
Phone: 555-5555
Office Hours: M 11:00 to 12:00, W 2:00 to 3:00, and by appointment
Virtual Office Hours: vaught@college.edu

[Teaching assistants, listed with e-mail addresses, office, office hours]

Course Description and Objectives
This course surveys modern American history from the latter third of the nine-teenth century to the present, using three complementary approaches: lecture, reading, and discussion. We will explore economic, social, cultural, and political developments, paying close attention to regional variations and the different experiences of whites and blacks, men and women, natives and immigrants, and workers and farmers. The objective is to be neither comprehensive nor defini-tive, but to introduce students to the key themes, events, and personalities of the period and to develop their critical thinking, writing, reading, and note-taking skills. Prerequisites: none.

Required Readings (available at the bookstore)
Thomas Bell, *Out of This Furnace: A Novel of Immigrant Labor in America*
John Kasson, *Amusing the Million: Coney Island at the Turn of the Century*
Sinclair Lewis, *Babbitt*
Yoshiko Uchida, *Desert Exile: The Uprooting of a Japanese-American Family*
Melba Pattillo Beals, *Warriors Don't Cry: A Searing Memoir of the Battle to
    Integrate Little Rock's Central High*
Philip Caputo, *A Rumor of War*
OPTIONAL TEXT: James A. Henretta, David Brody, and Lynn Dumenil,
    America: A Concise History, 3rd ed.

Assessment

All graded assignments and exams must be completed to earn a passing grade.

First Exam	10%	First Paper	15%
Second Exam	15%	Second Paper	25%
Final Exam	25%	Discussion	10%

Discussions

In the third hour of every week, students will meet in small discussion sections to explore issues and problems raised by the readings and to develop critical thinking, reading, and writing skills. (Some of you meet on Wednesdays, some on Thursdays, and some on Fridays.) Though your TA will facilitate these discussions, the burden of their success or usefulness is on you. It is very important, therefore, that students begin reading and thinking carefully about the books *well in advance* of the day of the discussion (see schedule below). Reading guides consisting of 10 to 15 questions will be distributed approximately two weeks prior to the discussion date. Answer the questions informally (a couple or so sentences for each) and note the approximate page numbers on which you find the answers. *Make a copy of your answers for yourself, and hand the original in at the beginning of the discussion section.* This will allow you to make additions while sharing your thoughts with your classmates. The reading guides will help prepare you for discussions, which in turn will help prepare you for papers and exams. Small discussion sections are rare at large universities like this one. Take advantage of this opportunity!

Papers

1.   First Paper: 15% of final grade
     A 3-page analytical essay based primarily on *one* of the first three required readings, due as follows:
     Bell, *Out of This Furnace*, due Feb. 2
     Kasson, *Amusing the Million*, due Feb. 16
     Lewis, *Babbitt*, due March 9
2.   Second Paper: 25% of final grade
     A 3-page analytical essay based primarily on *one* of the three remaining required readings, due as follows:
     Uchida, *Desert Exile*, due March 30
     Beals, *Warriors Don't Cry*, due April 20
     Caputo, *A Rumor of War*, due May 4

Topics will be distributed approximately two weeks prior to the due date. It is always wise to keep a copy of each written assignment until you receive your final grade. *When turning in papers, students should submit both paper and electronic copies to their teaching assistants.*

Exams

All three exams (February 18, 19, or 20; April 1, 2, or 3; and May 11) will be closed-book and closed-note and will cover *all* lectures and readings. Each exam will have two parts. Part I will consist of 30 multiple-choice/true-false questions from the lectures, and Part II will be one essay question based on the pertinent books (Bell and Kasson for Exam I, Lewis and Uchida for Exam II, and Beals and Caputo for Exam III). Part I will count for 60 percent of the exam grade, and Part II will be worth 40 percent. Please note that Part I will cover the lectures, *not* the textbook. This makes it imperative that you attend class regularly and read the books carefully. There will be NO MAKEUPS except for students with university-excused absences (please see http://student-rules.tamu.edu/rule07.htm for current policy on university-excused absences). It is the responsibility of the student to confer with his/her teaching assistant to arrange a day for the makeup exam.

Attendance and Late Papers
Attendance in lecture and discussion section will be taken on a random basis at least six or seven times throughout the semester. You will not be penalized for *two* unexcused absences, but on the *third* and subsequent unexcused absences, your grade for the course will drop a full notch (i.e., from an A to a B, B to a C, etc.). Papers that are submitted late will receive a grade of zero except in the case of university-excused absences or by prior arrangement with the instructor or teaching assistant.

Please see http://student-rules.tamu.edu/rule07.htm for the current policy on university-excused absences. For illness- or injury-related absences of fewer than three days, a note from a health care professional confirming date and time of visit will be required in order to count the absence as university-excused; for absences of three days or more, the note must also contain the medical professional's confirmation that absence from class was necessary (see Rule 7.1.6.1).

Tips
Above all, try to stay focused and relaxed! The lectures, readings, and paper topics are challenging. *Do not expect to understand them fully right off the bat.* Take careful notes and review them after each class, give yourself plenty of time to read (and reread) the books, come prepared for discussion, and do not wait until the last minute to write your papers. If you find yourself confused, *do not hesitate to come see your TA (or me) during office hours!* You might want to seek out a note-taking buddy or two in case you have to miss class.

Course Schedule: Lecture and Discussion Topics
Jan. 21   Introduction
              The Industrial Revolution
DISCUSSION SECTION: Writing Workshop I
Jan. 26   The Industrial Revolution (continued)
Jan. 28   The American Frontier
DISCUSSION SECTION: Bell, *Out of This Furnace* (pp. 3–217 only)
Feb. 2   The Rise of the City
              Bell Paper Due
Feb. 4   Gilded-Age Politics
DISCUSSION SECTION: preparation for first exam

Feb. 9   Gilded-Age Politics (continued)
              The Progressive Era
Feb. 11   The Progressive Era (continued)
DISCUSSION SECTION: Kasson, *Amusing the Million*
Feb. 16   An Emerging World Power
              Kasson Paper Due
Feb. 18   An Emerging World Power (continued)
              Loose Ends
DISCUSSION SECTION: *FIRST EXAM*
Feb. 23   World War I
Feb. 25   World War I (continued)
              The 1920s
DISCUSSION SECTION: exams returned and discussed
Mar. 2   The 1920s (continued)
Mar. 4   The Great Depression
DISCUSSION SECTION: Lewis, *Babbitt*
Mar. 9   The Great Depression (continued)
              The New Deal
              Lewis Paper Due
Mar. 11   The New Deal (continued)
DISCUSSION SECTION: Writing Workshop II
Mar. 16–20   SPRING BREAK
Mar. 23   The New Deal's Impact on Society
Mar. 25   World War II
DISCUSSION SECTION: Uchida, *Desert Exile*
Mar. 30   World War II (continued)
              Uchida Paper Due
Apr. 1   TBA
DISCUSSION SECTION: *SECOND EXAM*
Apr. 6   Cold War America
Apr. 8   Cold War America (continued)
              Affluence and Its Contradictions
DISCUSSION SECTION: no discussion sections this week
Apr. 13   Affluence and Its Contradictions (continued)
Apr. 15   The Ascent of Liberalism—JFK
DISCUSSION SECTION: Beals, *Warriors Don't Cry*
Apr. 20   The Civil Rights Movement and the Great Society
              Beals Paper Due
Apr. 22   The Continuing Struggle for Civil Rights
DISCUSSION SECTION: preparation for final exam
Apr. 27   Vietnam
Apr. 29   Vietnam (continued)
DISCUSSION SECTION: Caputo, *A Rumor of War*
May 4   Watergate and the Politics of Cynicism
              Caputo Paper Due
May 11   *FINAL EXAM*, Monday, 10:30 to 12:30, *in the lecture hall,*
              CHEM 100

Important Note

The handouts used in this course are copyrighted. By "handouts," I mean all materials generated for this class, which include, but are not limited to, syllabi, exams, reading guides, and paper topics. Because these materials are copyrighted, you do not have the right to copy the handouts, unless I expressly grant permission. Also, *please do not record the lectures or take notes for any outside note-taking company without my permission.*

Disabilities

The Americans with Disabilities Act (ADA) is a federal anti-discrimination statute that provides comprehensive civil rights protection for persons with disabilities. Among other things, this legislation requires that all students with disabilities be guaranteed a learning environment that provides for reasonable accommodation of their disabilities. If you believe you have a disability requiring an accommodation, please contact the Office of Support Services for Students with Disabilities in Room B-118 Cain Hall (123-4567).

Academic Integrity

"An Aggie does not lie, cheat, or steal, or tolerate those who do." You are expected to be aware of the Aggie Honor Code and the Honor Council Rules and Procedures, stated at http://www.tamu.edu/aggiehonor.

Guidelines for Writing Papers

Vaught's Ten Commandments

1. Papers *must* be typed or word-processed in standard-size (12-point) font, double-spaced, and with one-inch margins on all sides. *No exceptions!*
2. Proofread your papers carefully for spelling, grammar, and proper sentence and paragraph structure. Poor spelling and grammar will lower your grade significantly.
3. Do not use slang, contractions, abbreviations, or colloquialisms. Your own voice should come across in your papers.
4. Avoid the first person—i.e., "I," "I think," "in my opinion," etc. Avoid as well such phrases as "This paper will argue . . ."
5. Remember, this is a history class. When in doubt, use the past tense. And make sure you maintain a sense of time and change.
6. *Please* do not enclose your papers in any kind of folder or binder. One staple in the left-hand corner will do just fine. You need not include a title page. Simply type your name, date, course title, and section number in the upper right-hand corner. Your papers should include a title, however; center it before your first paragraph.
7. The grader will not read pages that go beyond the assigned length of the papers. Please do not exceed what I have specified.
8. Write simply, concisely, and interestingly. Remember that someone will be reading your papers. If you write something that you yourself would not enjoy reading, you can bet that your reader probably will not enjoy it either.
9. You should *not* assume that your reader has read the material or heard the lectures. *Anyone* should be able to understand your papers (though

someone having read the materials would no doubt appreciate their content at a deeper level). It is always a good idea to have one of your peers—your roommate, for example—read your papers and provide feedback.

10. **DO NOT PLAGIARIZE!** As commonly defined, plagiarism consists of passing off as one's own ideas, words, writings, etc., which belong to another. In accordance with this definition, you are committing plagiarism if you copy the work of another person and turn it in as your own, even if you have the permission of that person. Penalties are severe, including failing the course and expulsion from the university. If you have any doubt whatsoever about whether or not something constitutes plagiarism, **don't do it**. When turning in papers, *students should submit both paper and electronic copies*. Teaching assistants will then forward electronic copies to turnitin.com, an anti-plagiarism computer program that scans papers against every known Internet source, including other papers submitted to the site.

The Central Theme (or thesis statement)

1. The papers are designed to test and increase your abilities to analyze and argue. *You must take a position.*

2. Your argument, or central theme, should be stated explicitly and concisely in your opening paragraph. Each succeeding paragraph should in some way support the argument that you are making. Statements or paragraphs that do not in some way pertain to your central theme probably do not belong in the paper. In formulating your central theme, do not simply restate the question or simply state that a problem exists. You need to elaborate on the nature of the problem and indicate what your own position will be.

3. The central theme is the crucial part of your papers. Stated properly, it will provide structure to your essay. Stated unclearly or inadequately, it is likely that your paper will be unclear and inadequate as well. Remember, the less your reader has to struggle to understand your paper, the more likely he/she will appreciate its content.

4. One rarely develops a strong thesis statement right off the bat. Often, in fact, a writer figures out his/her central theme only after completing a first draft. In many papers, in fact, the thesis statement ends up in the conclusion. A paper is not like a movie, however. Do not keep your reader hanging in suspense until the end.

5. If you are in the habit of writing your papers in a single sitting just before they are due, you are denying yourself the pleasure of discovering your true writing abilities. Everything happens *after* the first draft. If you simply write down your first impressions and turn them in, most of your reading and thinking will have gone to waste. Even one additional hour of rethinking and rewriting will improve your paper immensely.

Paper and Paragraph Structure

1. Your papers should have the following features:
   Introduction (including the central theme)

The major points you will make in support of your central theme
Supporting evidence you will use to prove these points
Conclusion

2.   Generally, each major point should be stated in a single paragraph. Within
each paragraph, the opening (or topic) sentence should state the theme of
the paragraph, and each succeeding sentence should support this theme
in some way. Often, paragraph size demonstrates how well you have
organized your paper. A series of short (one or two sentences) paragraphs
means you are listing ideas, rather than developing them; and long (a page
or more) paragraphs mean you are running several ideas together, or just
rambling in general.

Reading, Writing, and Speaking

When reading books and articles for this and other classes, be conscious of how
the author organizes and presents his/her thoughts and materials. Why does the
work of one author appeal to you more than that of another?

It is also a good idea to read your paper aloud—either to yourself, a friend,
or a pet. You will hear awkward phrasing and unclear sentences that otherwise
you might not catch. Take your writing seriously. If you do not, you should not
expect others to do so.

History of the United States to 1877

For HIST 105, History of the United States to 1877, I employ the same format,
structure, and scheme as for HIST 106, with the following required readings and
course schedule:

Required Readings (available at the bookstore)
Kenneth Lockridge, *A New England Town*
Winthrop Jordan, *The White Man's Burden*
Robert Gross, *The Minutemen and Their World*
Paul Johnson, *A Shopkeeper's Millennium*
Harriet Jacobs, *Incidents in the Life of a Slave Girl*
Stephen Oates, *Abraham Lincoln: The Man Behind the Myths*
OPTIONAL TEXT: James A. Henretta, David Brody, and Lynn Dumenil,
    America: A Concise History, 3rd ed.

Course Schedule: Lecture and Discussion Topics
Aug. 31   Introduction
Sept. 2   The Meetings of Three Worlds: Native Americans
DISCUSSION SECTION: Reading and Writing Workshop I
Sept. 7   The Meetings of Three Worlds: Europeans and Africans
Sept. 9   The Northern Colonies: The Puritan Experience

DISCUSSION SECTION: Lockridge, *A New England Town*

Sept. 14   The Northern Colonies: Settlement, Cities, and Women
               Lockridge Paper Due

Sept. 16   Colonizing the South

DISCUSSION SECTION: preparation for first exam

Sept. 21   From Servitude to Slavery

Sept. 23   The Enlightenment and the Great Awakening

DISCUSSION SECTION: Jordan, *The White Man's Burden*

Sept. 28   Government, Politics, and Empire
               Jordan Paper Due

Sept. 30   The Road to Rebellion, 1763–1775

DISCUSSION SECTION: *FIRST EXAM*

Oct. 5   Making a New Republic

Oct. 7   The Constitution

DISCUSSION SECTION: exams returned and discussed

Oct. 12   The Republic in Crisis

Oct. 14   The Growth of the Slave South, Part I

DISCUSSION SECTION: Gross, *The Minutemen and Their World*

Oct. 19   The Growth of the Slave South, Part II
               Gross Paper Due

Oct. 21   The North's "Great Transformation," Part I

DISCUSSION SECTION: Reading and Writing Workshop II

Oct. 26   The North's "Great Transformation," Part II

Oct. 28   Democratizing Politics

DISCUSSION SECTION: Johnson, *A Shopkeeper's Millennium*

Nov. 2   Democratizing Culture
               Johnson Paper Due

Nov. 4   Lowell Mill Workers

DISCUSSION SECTION: *SECOND EXAM*

Nov. 9   Life in the Slave Quarters

Nov. 11   Slavery and the Beginnings of Sectional Conflict

DISCUSSION SECTION: exams returned and discussed

Nov. 16   Slavery and Westward Expansion

Nov. 18   The 1850s: Compromise and Conflict

DISCUSSION SECTION: Jacobs, *Incidents in the Life of a Slave Girl*

Nov. 23   The Civil War, Part I
               Jacobs Paper Due

Nov. 25   TBA

THANKSGIVING: No discussion sections

Nov. 30   The Civil War, Part II

Dec. 2   Reconstruction

DISCUSSION SECTION: Oates, *Abraham Lincoln*

Dec. 7   Redefined Day—No Class
               Oates Paper Due (to your teaching assistant)

Dec. 16   *THIRD EXAM*, Wednesday, 10:30 to 12:30, *in the lecture hall,*
               CHEM 100

Reading Guides

HIST 105, History of the United States to 1877

Reading Guide
Kenneth A. Lockridge, *A New England Town* (through p. 164 only)
As you read through the book, consider the following questions and issues:

1. What is Lockridge's objective, as outlined in the introduction?
2. Did the Dedham settlers see a contradiction between hierarchy and harmony in their community? Why or why not?
3. Why did the original Dedham settlers divide only 3,000 acres (less than 5 square miles) among themselves when they were granted 200 square miles? What does that say about their attitudes and values?
4. Dedham, according to Lockridge, was a "Christian Utopian Closed Corporate Community" (p. 16). Explain. How does this counter conventional wisdom regarding early New England settlement?
5. What was the "half-way" covenant, and why, according to Lockridge, was it implemented?
6. Dedham's political life "was a thing unto itself, full of contradictions which the modern mind is hard put to resolve but which were no contradictions at all to the mind of the seventeenth century" (p. 38). Explain.
7. In what ways was Dedham society "unmistakably 'American'" (p. 75)? In what ways was it not?
8. "Dedham's age of utopian communalism contained within itself the seeds of change" (p. 79). Explain.
9. In the late seventeenth and early eighteenth centuries, Dedham's largely subsistence economy remained essentially the same, and its relatively classless society remained intact as well. What, then, accounted for the "uneasy tension" (p. 117) that gripped the community by the end of the seventeenth century?
10. Compare the town meeting of the early 1700s to that of Dedham's earlier utopian age. Which was more "aristocratic"? What development above all others, according to Lockridge, accounted for the fact that Dedham residents "changed their political behavior" (p. 135)?
11. Describe the two "contradictions" (pp. 136–38) Lockridge sees in Dedham's maturing society at the turn of the eighteenth century.
12. How, as Lockridge suggests, might the social, religious, and political developments of Dedham's first one hundred years have influenced the American Revolution some forty years later?

Winthrop Jordan, *The White Man's Burden* (through p. 122 only)
As you read through the book, consider the following questions and issues:

1. Why, as depicted in the preface, does Jordan use the term *racism* reluctantly?
2. What did the concept of "blackness" mean to the British prior to American colonization?
3. What were Englishmen's initial impressions — religious, social, and sexual — of Africans before they became slaves in the American colonies?
4. What does Jordan mean by the "unthinking decision" (Chapter 2) to enslave Africans in America in the seventeenth century?
5. How did the terms *servant* and *slave* differ in seventeenth-century America and England?
6. As Jordan sees it, which came first, racism or slavery (see especially pp. 45, 54)?
7. What were slave codes, and what was their function, according to Jordan? Were they aimed at disciplining black men or white men?
8. Describe the tensions involved in miscegenation in the English colonies. What do these tensions tell us about racism and slavery in America?
9. "The white man's fears of Negro sexual aggression were equally apparent in the use of castration as a punishment in the colonies" (p. 81). Explain.
10. How did the colonists' religious beliefs impact their beliefs about slavery?
11. How did the concept of the "Great Chain of Being" allow colonists to rationalize slavery?
12. How and why, according to Jordan, did colonists differentiate between American Indians and African slaves?

Robert Gross, *The Minutemen and Their World* (through p. 170 only)
As you read through the book, consider the following questions and issues:

1. What does Gross mean by history "from the bottom up" (p. viii)? How does that focus affect his interpretation of the American Revolution?
2. How did the Great Awakening affect social and public life in Concord?
3. Compare Concord's pre–Revolutionary War politics to politics in College Station (or any comparable city) today.
4. Why, according to Gross, were Concordians so "reluctant" to oppose the Stamp Act?
5. What legislative act ultimately provoked the majority of Concordians to voice opposition to British imperial policy? What were Concordians trying to restore?
6. Did Concordians believe in democracy by 1775? If not, how would you characterize their political beliefs?
7. In what ways, according to Gross, was the makeup of Concord's Minutemen significant? Were their intentions radical?
8. How did land, poverty, and slavery affect Concord men and women on the eve of the Revolution? Explain why the "Revolution was a family affair" (p. 108) for the Barretts, the Browns, and the Hosmers.

9. Describe the hardships of war encountered by Concordians.
10. How, according to Gross, did the "social meaning of war" (p. 147) change over time?

Paul Johnson, *A Shopkeeper's Millennium* (read Chapters 3 and 4 very quickly)
As you read through the book, consider the following questions and issues:

1. What is Johnson's purpose in this book? What is he trying to explain?
2. Why does he choose Rochester, New York, for his setting? Why not New York City, for example?
3. What does Johnson mean when he describes Rochester as "a remarkably orderly and closed community of entrepreneurs" (p. 22)?
4. Who, according to Johnson, was most likely to join the Rochester churches in the early 1830s? How does this challenge other theories of why people respond to revival crusades?
5. With the emergence of industrial capitalism in the late 1820s and early 1830s, what were the most important changes in the conditions of work and in the relationships between employers and employees in Rochester—in shoemaking, for example?
6. How did reorganization of work affect households in Rochester?
7. What does Johnson mean by saying that in 1820 "there were no neighborhoods" (p. 48) in Rochester? How had this changed by the mid-1830s, and with what results?
8. Why did a "drinking problem" emerge in Rochester in the late 1820s? For whom was it a problem?
9. What was the most significant effect, according to Johnson, of the rise of both Antimasonry and the temperance crusade in Rochester? (Be sure not to let yourself get bogged down in the details of Chapters 3 and 4.)
10. What does Johnson mean when he asserts that "churchgoing businessmen had lost faith in their ability to govern" (p. 93) by 1830?
11. How did Charles Finney's message—"God has made man a moral free agent" (p. 1)—help businessmen retain their sense of social order?
12. What does it mean to say that shopkeepers "experienced disobedience and disorder as religious problems" (p. 140)?
13. Do any significant groups seem to be neglected from Johnson's analysis?

Harriet Jacobs, *Incidents in the Life of a Slave Girl*
As you read through the book, consider the following questions and issues:

1. In writing this narrative, what did Jacobs wish to achieve?
2. Why, do you think, did Harriet Jacobs use an alias in her narrative? If they were her experiences, why not just use her own name?
3. What do you find striking or unexpected about Linda Brent's childhood? After you've finished the book, reread this chapter and ask yourself the same question again. In fact, you ought to do this with all the questions.
4. What significance did New Year's Day have for Jacobs?

5. Why was the fifteenth year, in Jacobs's words, "a sad epoch in the life of a slave girl" (p. 27)? Contrast this to how you would imagine the fifteenth year of a daughter about to embark upon middle-class "true womanhood" (pure, pious, domestic, submissive).

6. "The secrets of slavery are concealed like those of the Inquisition" (p. 35). Explain, especially in regard to Mrs. Flint.

7. "Why does the slave ever love" (p. 37)? How did Jacobs answer her own question?

8. Why did Jacobs dwell so much on sexual relations—in Chapters 9, 10, and throughout the book? Pay particular attention to her language, as on p. 54, for example.

9. Why did Linda Brent bemoan the fact that her newborn child was a girl?

10. "My master had power and law on his side; I had a determined will. There is might in each" (p. 85). Explain. How did Linda Brent exert power over Dr. Flint?

11. What dilemma did Linda Brent's children pose for her? What effect would this have on Jacobs's readers?

12. What elements of slave culture did Jacobs present to her readers, and for what purpose?

13. "Slavery perverted all the natural feelings of the human heart." Explain, and again, pay close attention to Jacobs's language.

14. "There are no bonds so strong as those which are formed by suffering together" (p. 170). How might a northern middle-class woman have responded to such a statement?

Stephen B. Oates, *Abraham Lincoln: The Man Behind the Myths*

As you read through the book, consider the following questions and issues:

1. What are the principal problems of Carl Sandburg's epic biography of Lincoln, according to Oates?

2. What value, if any, do "Lincoln myths" hold for us, according to Oates?

3. How did Lincoln's "log-cabin origins" affect him?

4. Why, in Oates's estimation, would a man like Lincoln—a man prone to deep depressions and obsessions with death—seek a life in politics, a life so open to the public eye?

5. How does the "complex, richly human Lincoln" (p. 54) portrayed by Oates differ from the "Plain and Humble Man of the People" myth and the "Arch Villain" myth that previous biographers have given us?

6. What made Lincoln "detest" slavery from a very early age? What was his early "solution" to this "relic of despotism" (pp. 60–61)?

7. If Lincoln detested slavery, why did he shy away from the abolitionist movement?

8. Why did the Kansas-Nebraska Act upset Lincoln so much?

9. What does Oates mean when he writes that Lincoln saw the slavery problem "in a world dimension" (p. 75)?

10. Why was the Fort Sumter crisis a "rude awakening" (p. 84) for Lincoln?
11. "The story of emancipation could well be called the liberation of Abraham Lincoln" (p. 112). Explain.
12. Would Reconstruction have been different had Lincoln lived, according to Oates?
13. What does Oates mean by writing that "we have never again been the same" (p. 169) since Lincoln's assassination?

HIST 106, History of the United States from 1877

Reading Guide
Thomas Bell, *Out of This Furnace* (pp. 3–217 only)
As you read through the book, consider the following questions and issues:

1. What factors prompted George Kracha to leave Hungary for the coal fields of northwestern Pennsylvania? Were these factors typical for turn-of-the-century central and southern European immigrants?
2. What is married life like for Kracha and Elena?
3. What strikes you most about work in the steel mills?
4. Based on the problems Kracha encounters—his arrival, his affair, the deaths of his two friends—how would you characterize him? Does he seem to have much control over his life? Who (or what) do you think Bell is blaming for the plight of the characters in the novel?
5. Are there elements in Slovak life that Bell seems to downplay?
6. What role do women play in the novel?
7. What sorts of discrimination do the Dobrejcaks face?
8. Compare the dreams and aspirations of Kracha to those of Mike Dobrejcak. Does either character achieve their more fanciful dreams? Their more realistic dreams?
9. Consider the other generational comparisons as outlined in the paper topic.
10. Would you characterize the solutions that Kracha, Mike, and other Slavic immigrants in this book pursue to solve their problems as individualistic or collective?
11. In the last part of the book, which I encourage you to read when you get the chance, Bell depicts the efforts of third-generation immigrants to unionize in the 1930s. Based on your perceptions of the first two generations, do you believe those efforts will succeed?

John Kasson, *Amusing the Million*
As you read through the book, consider the following questions and issues:

1. Why, according to Kasson, is Coney Island at the turn of the century significant for more than just the nostalgia that it arouses?
2. "Amusement parks served as laboratories of the new mass culture" (p. 8). Explain.

3. What was Frederick Law Olmsted's main purpose in designing New York's Central Park?

4. In what way was the Columbian Exposition similar to Central Park? In what way was it different?

5. What conclusion does Kasson draw from the photograph of the crowd at the Columbian Exposition on p. 22? Do you agree?

6. Why, according to Kasson, was the response to Coney Island both "immediate and overwhelming" (p. 36) among immigrants, working-class visitors, and the rising middle class alike?

7. "Coney Island has a code of conduct which is all her own" (p. 41). Explain the significance of this contemporary observation.

8. What does the photograph on p. 49 suggest about Coney Island, according to Kasson?

9. What do the amusement parks that Kasson analyzes have in common with amusement parks today? How do they differ?

10. What does Kasson conclude about the difference between the photograph on p. 93 and the picture on p. 92? What did social critic James Gibbons Huneker think about it?

11. "Face-to-face communities provided important checks on behavior; by contrast, the anonymous life of the metropolis appeared to leave individuals rootless and unrestrained" (p. 98). Explain the significance of this statement to the Coney Island phenomenon.

12. In what way, according to Kasson, did Coney Island "arouse an ambivalence that went to the heart of progressive reform" (p. 104)? Did Coney Island signify "liberation" or "a new form of subjection" (p. 108)?

13. Do you think the character George Kracha from *Out of This Furnace* would have liked Coney Island? Why or why not?

Sinclair Lewis, *Babbitt*
As you read through the novel, consider the following questions and issues:

1. In the first two chapters, Lewis juxtaposes the "towers of Zenith" with Babbitt's less-than-thrilling personal and family life. Comment.

2. What does it say about Babbitt that he "respects bigness in anything" (p. 27)?

3. What were Babbitt's virtues as a "real-estate man"? How did those virtues shape his opinion of labor unions?

4. Analyze Babbitt's relationship with Paul Riesling. Why is he so loyal to "Old Paulibus"?

5. Where does Babbitt get his opinions about art and literature? What does that tell us about him?

6. "Fellow's own fault if he doesn't show the initiative to up and beat it to the city" (p. 105). Comment. How does Babbitt shape Zenith, and how does Zenith shape Babbitt?

7. How does Lewis portray women—Myra, Zilla, and Tanis? Are they as complacent as the men seem to be?

8. What does the train scene (pp. 124–30) tell us about Babbitt?
9. Does Babbitt enjoy his Maine vacation and other "relaxations"? Why or why not?
10. Examine Babbitt's speech to the Zenith Real Estate Board (pp. 161–69). What do his oratory skills and discourse tell us about him? What does he think about politics?
11. Why was Babbitt a "joiner" (p. 181)?
12. Was Babbitt a religious man? Why or why not?
13. What effect did Paul's troubles have on Babbitt? Does Babbitt have a conscience?
14. What do you make of the following response from a leading contemporary business journal to *Babbitt* in 1924? "Dare to be a Babbitt! What the world needs are more Babbitts, good Rotarians who live orderly lives, save money, go to church, play golf, and send their children to school."
15. Is Lewis at all optimistic about middle-class America in the 1920s, or should we consider *Babbitt* a tragedy?

Yoshiko Uchida, *Desert Exile*
As you read through the book, consider the following questions and issues:

1. How was Uchida's upbringing and family life similar to other American citizens? How was it different?
2. Analyze the differences between the two generations, the Issei (first) and the Nisei (second).
3. On p. 40, Uchida writes, "Neither my sister nor I, as children, ever considered ourselves anything but Americans." Yet, five pages later she says, "We were neither totally American nor totally Japanese, but a unique fusion of the two." How do you reconcile these two statements?
4. What did the U.S. government do to Uchida's father immediately after Pearl Harbor? Why? Where did his loyalties lie, with Japan or the United States?
5. What prompted the sentiment on the West Coast for the evacuation of Japanese Americans at the beginning of World War II? On what basis does Uchida claim that "the forced evacuation was carried out purely on the basis of race" (p. 57)?
6. Why did Uchida's mother enter Tanforan "dressed just as she would have been to go to church" (p. 69)?
7. What conditions did Japanese Americans face in the Tanforan "assembly center"? At the "relocation camp" at Topaz?
8. How did Japanese Americans organize themselves at Tanforan and Topaz? What motivated them to do so?
9. What effect did Topaz have on family life and on relations between Issei and Nisei?
10. Why, do you think, did Japanese Americans not rebel more against their treatment in the camps?
11. How could some Japanese leave the camps as early as 1942?

12. What kinds of support did whites give Japanese Americans just prior to, and during, their internment? Why did more not come to their aid?
13. Who do you think suffered more during internment, Issei or Nisei?

Melba Pattillo Beals, *Warriors Don't Cry*
As you read through the book, consider the following questions and issues:

1. What was it like for Beals at the thirty-year commemoration for the Little Rock Nine?
2. What examples of segregation do you find in the early chapters, and how did segregation make Beals feel as a child?
3. How did Beals become one of the Little Rock Nine? Why does she want to attend Central High School?
4. What role did the NAACP and the court system play in the process of integration in Little Rock and throughout the South? Who was the main public figure who fueled the anti-integration movement in Little Rock? What were his motivations?
5. Neither Beals nor her mother anticipated what would happen the first day she tried to attend Little Rock High. Why not? Why did she go back after what had happened?
6. In what ways did Beals's family, neighbors, friends, and church react to her integration efforts? From where did she draw her strength during the school year?
7. How did segregationists in Little Rock put pressure on blacks to abandon the integration efforts? In what ways did blacks respond?
8. How did white students treat Beals? How did her teachers and other school officials tend to react? How did she respond?
9. As the school year wore on, how did Beals change—physically, spiritually, and emotionally?
10. How did the state troops treat Beals differently from the federal troops? What accounted for the differences?
11. Describe the importance of the following people to Beals during the year: Danny, Andy, Vince, Minnijean, Link.
12. What happened to the Little Rock schools after the first year of integration? What happened to Beals?
13. How did Beals's experiences at Central High influence her life? How would you characterize her, ultimately?

Philip Caputo, *A Rumor of War*
As you read through the book, consider the following questions and issues:

1. Why do you think Caputo insists that his memoir "ought not to be regarded as a protest" (p. xxi)?
2. Explain the meaning behind the title of Part One, "The Splendid Little War."
3. What reasons does Caputo cite for wanting to go to Vietnam?

4. What "moments of exhilaration" (p. 19) did Caputo experience during Officers' Basic School in the Marine Corps?
5. What impact did being "chewed out in front of the troops" (p. 34) at Camp Schwab have on Caputo? Compare that to how he felt when he first learned his battalion was "going South" (p. 40).
6. Explain the significance of the Vietnam War being "primarily a nocturnal event" (p. 56).
7. Why was the war so often "boring" and "phony" for Caputo and other soldiers? Explain what Caputo means by "la cafard."
8. "It was as though we were in an open-air theater, watching a war movie" (p. 71). Explain.
9. What does Caputo mean by "a formless war against a formless enemy" (p. 95)?
10. Explain the impact on Caputo of "the mutilation caused by modern weapons" (p. 128).
11. What was it like for Caputo to be "the Officer in Charge of the Dead"?
12. What impact did Sullivan's and Levy's deaths have on Caputo?
13. "Ethics seemed to be a matter of distance and technology" (pp. 229–30). Explain.
14. In what ways had Caputo's "gung-ho enthusiasm" (p. 260) changed from when he first came to Vietnam to when his platoon engaged in "Operation Harvest Moon"?
15. Explain the circumstances leading up to Caputo's "murder" trial. Why, in his mind, did not "the facts amount to the truth" (p. 330)?
16. How did Caputo react to his book's initial success?

Selected Lecture Outlines

HIST 105, History of the United States to 1877

The Meeting of Three Worlds: Europeans and Africans

I.   Crisis in Europe
    A. Gold
    B. The Breakdown of Feudal Society
        1. Agricultural Stagnation
        2. Peasant Revolts
    C. New Sources of Wealth and Labor
II. West Africa
    A. Culture and Economy
    B. The Slave Trade
    C. The South Atlantic System
III. Toward British Colonization
    A. Two Groups in Transition
    B. Peasants
        1. Cash Rents
        2. A "Just Price"
    C. Reorganization of the British Upper Classes
        1. Gentry
        2. Urban Merchants
        3. Enclosure
    D. The New World Solution

The Northern Colonies: The Puritan Experience

I.   Economic and Religious Origins
    A. John Winthrop and the Massachusetts Bay Company
    B. "Chosen People"
    C. Predestination
    D. Appeal
II. Settlement and Social Order
    A. Visible Saints
    B. "Little Commonwealths"
        1. The Meeting House
        2. Open Fields
        3. Land Ownership

III. Conflict and Dissent
    A. Samuel Sewall and the Supernatural
    B. The Salem Witch Trials
    C. Puritan-Indian Relations
        1. Disease
        2. Conquest — Pequot War
        3. Fur Trade

The Road to Rebellion, 1763–1775

I.   Attempts at Imperial Reorganization, 1763–1766
    A. The Treaty of Paris
    B. Debt and Pontiac's Rebellion
    C. The Proclamation of 1763
    D. The Sugar Act
    E. The Stamp Act
        1. Uproar
        2. Internal vs. External Taxes
II.   British Authority Disintegrates, 1767–1775
    A. The Townshend Act
        1. Glass, Lead, Paper, Paint, Tea
        2. The Boston Massacre
    B. The Tea Act
        1. The East India Tea Co.
        2. The Boston Tea Party
    C. The Coercive/Intolerable Acts
    D. The Quebec Act
    E. The First Continental Congress
    F. The Shot Heard 'Round the World
III. The British Perspective

The Constitution

I.   Off the Pedestal
II.   "The Imprudence of Democracy"
    A. 1776 vs. 1787
    B. The Articles of Confederation
        1. A Failed, but Noble, Experiment
        2. The Northwest Ordinance
III. The Philadelphia Convention, 1787
    A. A New (Albeit Illegal) Constitution
    B. Cutting a Political Deal
        1. The "Great Compromise"
        2. The Three-Fifths Compromise
IV. Ratification

    A. Federalists vs. Anti-Federalists
    B. *The Federalist*
    C. New York
    D. Why No Counterrevolution?

Slavery and Slave Culture

I.   From the Slaves' Perspective
II.   An Uphill Battle
    A. Subordinate Legal Status
    B. Complementary Interests with Masters
        1. Life Expectancy
        2. Population Growth
III. From Dusk to Dawn: Life in the Slave Quarters
    A. Family
        1. Marriage and Kinship
        2. Planter Wives and Miscegenation
    B. Religion: Slave Christianity
    C. Leisure
        1. Music and Dancing
        2. The "Trickster Tale"—Brer Rabbit
IV. Protest and Resistance
    A. Sabotage in the Fields
    B. Runaways
    C. Rebellion
        1. The Stono Rebellion
        2. Nat Turner, 1831
        3. Two Seminole Wars
    D. Contrast to the North

Reconstruction

I.   Issues, Actors, Characteristics
II.   The Meaning of Freedom
    A. Personal Expressions
    B. Opposition
        1. The Land Issue
        2. The Freedmen's Bureau
III. The Politics of Reconstruction
    A. Presidential Reconstruction
    B. Radical Reconstruction
        1. Civil Rights Act
        2. 14th Amendment
        3. Reconstruction Act of 1867
        4. Black Political Participation
        5. White Allies

    C. Planter "Redemption"
       1. Northern Retreat
       2. Ku Klux Klan
       3. Brief Counterattack
       4. Weariness Sets In
       5. Compromise of 1877
       6. "You Gave Us No Acres"

HIST 106, History of the United States from 1877

The Industrial Revolution (75 Minutes)

I.   1877
II. The Rise of Industrial Capitalism
    A. Consumer vs. Capital Goods
    B. Steel
       1. Bessemer Converters
       2. Andrew Carnegie
    C. Reforming the Railroad System
    D. Gustavus Swift and Vertical Integration
III. Victims
    A. Local Merchants
    B. Wage Earners
       1. "New" Immigrants
       2. Craft Workers
       3. Mass Production
       4. Frederick Winslow Taylor
    C. The Labor Movement and Industrial Warfare
       1. The Paradox of the AFL
       2. The Homestead Strike
       3. The Pullman Boycott
    D. The Failure of the New South

The American Frontier

I.   Farm and Factory
II. Life on the Great Plains
    A. A "Frontier Wasteland"?
    B. Buffalo and the Sioux
    C. The Railroad Catalyst
    D. Cattle Ranching — Boom and Bust
    E. Farming
       1. "The Rain Follows the Plow"
       2. Hazards and Advantages
       3. Dry Farming
    F. "Nature's Metropolis"

III. Farming East of the 98th Meridian
    A. Market-Oriented Agriculture
    B. Discontent
        1. Farm Life
        2. The Grange
        3. Economic Grievances
        4. Deflation

The Progressive Era (75 Minutes)

I. Crisis and Reform
II. Progressivism
    A. Intellectual Roots
        1. Idealism and Religion
        2. Muckrakers
    B. Political Reforms
        1. Municipal—The Galveston Plan
        2. State—La Follette and "Direct Democracy"
    C. Women Progressives
        1. Jane Addams and the Settlement House
        2. Suffrage and Feminism
    D. The South
III. National Politics
    A. TR: A Progressive President
        1. "That Damn Cowboy"
        2. 1902 Coal Strike
        3. Trusts, Sherman Antitrust Act, Trust Busting
        4. "Square Deal" Politics
        5. Taft
        6. The New Nationalism
    B. Woodrow Wilson and the New Freedom
        1. 1912
        2. Clayton Antitrust Act
        3. Corporate Liberalism

World War One (75 Minutes)

I. The Globalization of America
II. The "Great War"
    A. Failed Alliances
    B. Technology
    C. Neutrality
        1. U-Boats and the *Lusitania*
        2. "Safe for Democracy"
    D. "Over There"
        1. Conscription
        2. Allied Victory

III. The Home Front
    A. Business and Industry
        1. Government Intrusion
        2. Food Administration
        3. War Industries Board
    B. Workers
        1. National War Labor Board
        2. Women
    C. Unity and Dissent
IV. An Unsettled Peace
    A. The Treaty of Versailles
        1. Wilson's 14 Points—League of Nations
        2. Opposition and Defeat
    B. Social Tensions
        1. Racial Strife—Chicago
        2. Labor Unrest—Steel
        3. The Red Scare—Palmer Raids

The Great Depression

I. A National, Global, and Personal Matter
II. Causes
    A. The Stock Market Crash
    B. Structural Weaknesses
III. Hard Times
    A. Despair and Humiliation
    B. Women's Experiences
    C. Blacks' Experiences
        1. The Scottsboro Case
        2. Harlem
    D. The Dust Bowl
        1. Causes
        2. "Okies"
IV. The Political Response
    A. Blaming Hoover/Resurrecting Hoover
    B. Discontent and Rebellion
        1. Farm Holiday Association
        2. Bonus Army
    C. The 1932 Election

The Cold War, 1945–1960 (75 Minutes)

I. A Different Sort of War
II. The Early Years
    A. Sources of Conflict
        1. U.S. Strengths and Soviet Weaknesses
        2. Atomic Diplomacy

    B. Truman and Stalin
       1. Different Understandings of the Past
       2. Containment — the Truman Doctrine
       3. Marshall Plan
       4. Czechoslovakia and Berlin
       5. NATO and the Warsaw Pact
       6. China
       7. NSC-68
       8. Korean War
III. The Great Fear
    A. HUAC
    B. Alger Hiss
    C. Rise and Fall of Senator McCarthy
IV. Eisenhower
    A. Dulles and "Rollback"
    B. Khrushchev and Hungary
    C. "More Bang for the Buck"
    D. Alliances and Interventions — the CIA
    E. MAD
    F. Military-Industrial Complex

Watergate and the Politics of Cynicism

I.   Getting Caught
II.   The 1972 Election
    A. Democratic Self-Destruction
    B. A Nixon Landslide
III. Watergate
    A. Stretching the Boundaries of Law
    B. The Pentagon Papers
    C. Plumbers, Enemies, "Dirty Tricks," and CREEP
    D. The Break-In and Cover-Up
    E. Investigations, Hearings, and Tapes
    F. The Final Days
    G. Aftermath
    H. Our Dilemma